THE CLASSIFICATION OF THIS PUBLICATION HAS BEEN
CHANGED FROM RESTRICTED TO UNCLASSIFIED.

AN 01-190EB-1

GRUMMAN TBF/TBM-3 AVENGER PILOT'S FLIGHT OPERATING INSTRUCTIONS

THIS PUBLICATION SUPERSEDES AN 01-190EB-1 DATED 15 AUGUST 1945

PUBLISHED UNDER JOINT AUTHORITY OF THE COMMANDING GENERAL,
ARMY AIR FORCES AND THE CHIEF OF THE BUREAU OF AERONAUTICS

This manual is sold for historic research purposes only, as an entertainment.
It is not intended to be used as part of an actual flight training program. No
book can substitute for flight training by an authorized instructor. The licensing
of pilots is overseen by organizations and authorities such as the FAA and CAA.
Operating an aircraft without the proper license is a federal crime.

©2006-2010 PERISCOPE FILM LLC
ALL RIGHTS RESERVED
ISBN #978-1-935700-37-1

WWW.PERISCOPEFILM.COM

1 November 1945

AN 01-190-EB-1

Reproduction of the information or illustrations contained in this handbook or catalog is not permitted without specific approval of the issuing service (War or Navy Department).

LIST OF REVISED PAGES ISSUED

NOTE.—A heavy black vertical line, in the outer margin of revised pages (the left margin for left-hand columns, and the right margin for right-hand columns) indicates the extent of the revision. This line is omitted where more than 50 percent of the page is revised. A black horizontal line to the left of the page numbers listed below indicates pages revised, added or deleted by current revision. The line is used only on second and subsequent revisions.

BuAer

Additional Copies of This Publication May Be Obtained as Follows:

AAF ACTIVITIES.—In accordance with AAF Regulation No. 5-9.

NAVY ACTIVITIES.—Submit request to nearest supply point listed below, using form NavAer-140:
NAS, Alameda, Calif.; ASD, Orote, Guam; NAS, Jacksonville, Fla.; NAS, Norfolk, Va.; NASD, Oahu: NASD, Philadelphia, Pa.; NAS, San Diego, Calif.; NAS, Seattle, Wash.

For complete listing of available material and details of distribution see Naval Aeronautics Publications Index, NavAer 00-500.

AN 01-190EB-1

TABLE OF CONTENTS

SECTION I
DESCRIPTION

	PAGE
1. Airplane	1
a. General Description	1
b. Protection from Gunfire	2
c. Hydraulic System	2
d. Electrical System	7
2. Power Plant	9
a. Engine	9
b. Propeller	9
c. Oil System	9
d. Fuel System	9
3. Controls	12
a. Airplane Controls	12
b. Power Plant Controls	13
c. Alighting Gear	16
d. Wing Flaps	18
e. Wing Folding and Spreading Controls	19
4. Movement of Personnel	19

SECTION II
NORMAL OPERATING INSTRUCTIONS

	PAGE
1. Before Entering Pilot's Compartment	28
a. Flight Limitations and Restrictions	28
b. Weight and Balance	29
c. Access to Airplane	29
2. On Entering the Cockpit	29
a. Pilot's Seat	29
b. Wing Spreading and Folding	29
c. Standard Check for all Flights	30
d. Special Check for Night Flights	30
3. Fuel System Management	30
a. Procedure to Use When Changing Tanks	30
b. Order in Which to Use Tanks	30
4. Starting Engine	31
5. Engine Warm-Up	31
6. Engine Ground Test	32
7. Taxiing Instructions	32
8. Emergency Take-Off	33
9. Take-Off	33
a. Normal Take-Off	33
b. Minimum Take-Off	33
c. Catapult Take-Off	33
10. Engine Failure During Take-Off	33
11. Climb	34
12. General Flying Characteristics	34
a. Airplane	34
b. Engine	34

SECTION II—Cont.

	PAGE
13. Maneuvers Prohibited	35
14. Stalls	36
15. Spins	36
16. Acrobatics	36
17. Diving	36
18. Approach and Landing	36
a. Check-Off List	36
b. Power Plant Controls	36
c. Carrier Operation	37
19. Stopping Engine	37
20. Use of Oil Dilution System	37
a. General	37
b. Procedure	37
c. Precautions	38
21. Use of the Carburetor Induction System	38
22. Night Flying	38
23. Before Leaving Airplane	38

SECTION III
FLIGHT OPERATING DATA

	PAGE
1. Power Plant Chart	40
2. Airspeed Installation Correction	42

SECTION IV
EMERGENCY OPERATIONS

	PAGE
1. Power Plant Failure in Flight	43
2. Hydraulic System Failure	43
3. Ditching	43
4. Life Raft	44
5. Emergency Exits	45

SECTION V
OPERATIONAL EQUIPMENT

	PAGE
1. Middle Compartment	47
2. Bombardier's Compartment	48
a. General	48
b. Oxygen Equipment	48
c. Radio and Communications	49
d. Bombing Equipment	49
3. Turret	49
a. General	49
b. Electrical Controls	49
c. Manual Operating Equipment	50
d. Operation	50

AN 01-190EB-1

TABLE OF CONTENTS

SECTION V—Cont.

	PAGE
4. Oxygen System	50
a. General	50
b. Pre-Flight Check	51
c. Operating Instruction	51
5. Armament	52
a. General	52
b. Runaway Guns	53
c. Turret Gun	53
d. Wing Guns	54
e. Gun Sights and Cameras	55
f. Gun Packages	55
g. R. P. Installation	56
6. Communications, Navigation, Radar, and Special Service Equipment and Operation	57
a. Communication Equipment	57
b. Pilot's Instructions—Normal Operation of Controls from Warm-Up to Landing	60
c. Operation of AN/APS-4 Radar, AN/ARR-2 (IFF), and AN/APN-1 Altimeter Equipment (Operator Controlled)	64

SECTION V—Cont.

	PAGE
7. Automatic Pilot	68
a. General	68
b. Operation of Automatic Pilot	68
c. Condensed Operating Instructions	70
8. Bombing Equipment	71
a. General	71
b. Bombing Controls	71
c. Operation	74
d. Glide Bombing	76
9. Heating and Ventilating	77
10. Miscellaneous Equipment	77
a. Tow Target	77
b. Smoke Tank	78
c. Pyrotechnics	78
d. Chartboard	78
e. Relief Tubes	78

APPENDIX I

Take-Off, Climb, and Landing Chart	79
Flight Operating Instruction Charts	81
Engine Calibration Chart	85

TABLE OF ILLUSTRATIONS

FIGURE	PAGE
1. General Views of Airplane	Preface
2. Identification Silhouette	1
3. Principal Dimensions	2
4. Protection from Gunfire, Turret Position	3
4A. Protection from Gunfire, Pilot's Position	4
5. Hydraulic System Schematic Diagram	5
6. Hydraulic System	6
7. Hydraulic Pressure Gage	7
8. Landing Gear Hydraulic Circuit	7
9. Wing Flap Hydraulic Circuit	7
10. Wing Fold Spread and Lock Hydraulic Circuit	8
11. Wing Gun Charger Hydraulic Circuit	8

FIGURE	PAGE
12. Oil System	10
13. Fuel System	11
14. Stick and Harness	12
15. Elevator Trim Tab Control	12
16. Rudder Trim Tab Control	13
17. Aileron Trim Tab Control	13
18. Fuel Tank Selector	13
19. Auxilliary Fuel Pump Switch	14
20. Engine Control Quadrant	14
21. Carburetor Air Control	14
22. Cowl Flaps Control	15
23. Ignition Switch	15
24. Starter Switch	15

TABLE OF ILLUSTRATIONS—Cont.

FIGURE	PAGE
25. Starter Crank	15
26. Oil Cooler Flap Control	16
27. Propeller Control	16
28. Alighting Gear and Wing Flap Control	17
29. Arresting Hook Switch	18
29A. External Arresting Hook Control Handle	18A
30. Wing Folding and Spreading Controls	19
31. Wing Fold Warnings	19
32. Movements of Personnel	20
33. Pilot's Instrument Panel—Top Center	21
34. Pilot's Instrument Panel—Lower Center	21
35. Pilot's Instrument Panel—Lower Port	22
36. Pilot's Instrument Panel—Lower Starboard	22
37. Pilot's Cockpit—Port Side	23
38. Pilot's Sub Panel	23
39. Pilot's Cockpit Starboard Side	24
40. Pilot's Electrical Distribution Panel	25
41. Bombardier's Compartment—Front	26
42. Bombardier's Compartment—Port Side	27
43. Access to Cockpit	29
44. Wing Folding and Spreading	30
45. Temperature and Pressure Gage	31
46. Oil Dilution Switch	38
47. External Lights	39
48. Power Plant Chart	41
49. Airspeed Installation Correction Table	42
50. Pilot's Compartment Emergency Release	45
51. Bombardier's Compartment Emergency Release	45
52. Turret Emergency Release	45
53. Emergency Equipment and Exits	46
54. Middle Compartment	47
55. Turret	48
56. Turret Main Control Unit	49
57. Turret Switch Box and Switches	50
58. Oxygen Regulator	51

FIGURE	PAGE
59. Oxygen System	52
60. Angles of Gunfire	53
61. Mark 8 Sight	55
62. Deleted	56
62A R. P. Distribution Unit (Used on Earlier TBM-3 Airplanes)	56A
62B. R. P. Selector Switch (Used on Later TBM-3 Airplanes)	56A
63. Pilot's Radio Control Units	58
64. Pilot's Transmitter Control Unit	59
65. Receiver Tuning Head	59
66. Pilot's Receiver Control Unit	60
67. Pilot's AN/ARC-1 Control Unit	60
68. Pilot's AN/ARC-5 Control Unit	61
69. Operator's AN/ARC-5 Control Unit	61
70. Communications Equipment, Schematic	63
71. Deleted	64
72. IFF Pilot's Control	65
73. AN/APN-1 Altimeter Operation	66
74. Altimeter Controls and Indicator	67
75. Erratic Readings in a Steep Bank	67
76. Automatic Pilot Control and Hydraulic Gage	69
77. Automatic Pilot Control	70
78. 100 lb. Bomb Installation	72
79. 500 lb. Bomb Installation	73
80. 1000 lb. Bomb Installation	73
81. 1000 and 1600 lb. Bomb Installation	74
82. 2000 lb. Bomb Installation	75
83. Torpedo Installation	76
84. Smoke Tank Installation	77
84A Heater Installation, Earlier Model Airplanes	78A
84B Heater Installation, Later Model Airplanes	78A
85. Take-off, Climb, and Landing Chart	79
86. Flight Operating Instruction Chart	81
87. Engine Calibration Chart	85

AN 01-190EB-1

Figure 1 — TBM-3 Airplane

AN 01-190EB-1

SECTION I
DESCRIPTION

1. AIRPLANE

a. GENERAL DESCRIPTION. — The TBM-3 "AVENGER" is a single engine, midwing, all metal monoplane of semi-monocoque construction. It is designed as a torpedo bomber for carrier or land based operation.

The crew consists of three members, pilot, turret gunner who is also the radioman and a bombardier who is also the radar operator.

The wing is of full cantilever construction, with an outer panel folding arrangement of the stand-on-edge and fold-straight-back type.

Alighting gear is conventional and fully retractable.

The Wright Cyclone C-14BB (R-2600-20), 14 cylinder radial, double row, air cooled engine drives a three-blade Hamilton Standard Hydromatic Propeller. The engine is equipped with a single stage, gear driven, two-speed supercharger, and a Stromberg Injection Carburetor.

The over-all dimensions are as follows:

        Span......................54'2"
        Length (Three Point Atti-
            tude)..................39'5$\tfrac{11}{16}$"
        Height (tail up)...........16'5"
        Height (in normal position
            at rest)...............15'5$\tfrac{1}{32}$"
        Height (wings folded)......16'5"
        Width (wings folded)......19'
        Landing Gear Tread (width
            between tire centerlines) 10'10"

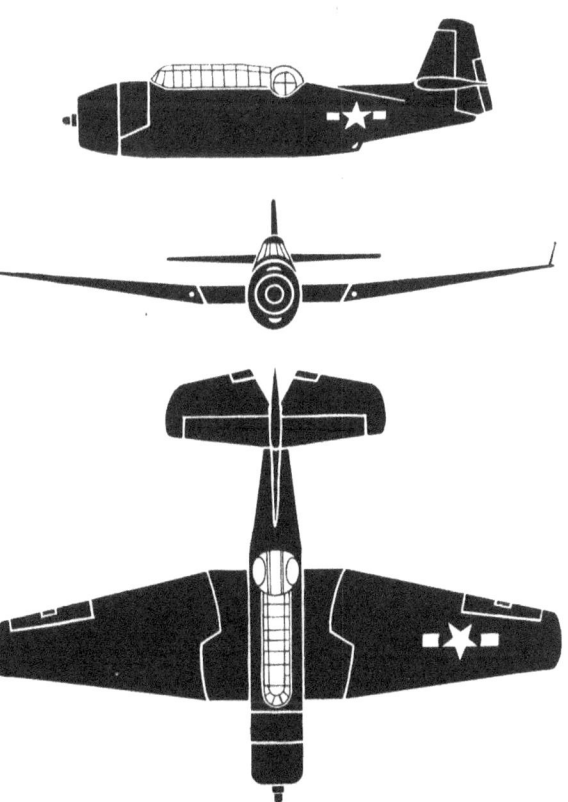

Figure 2 — Identification Silhouette

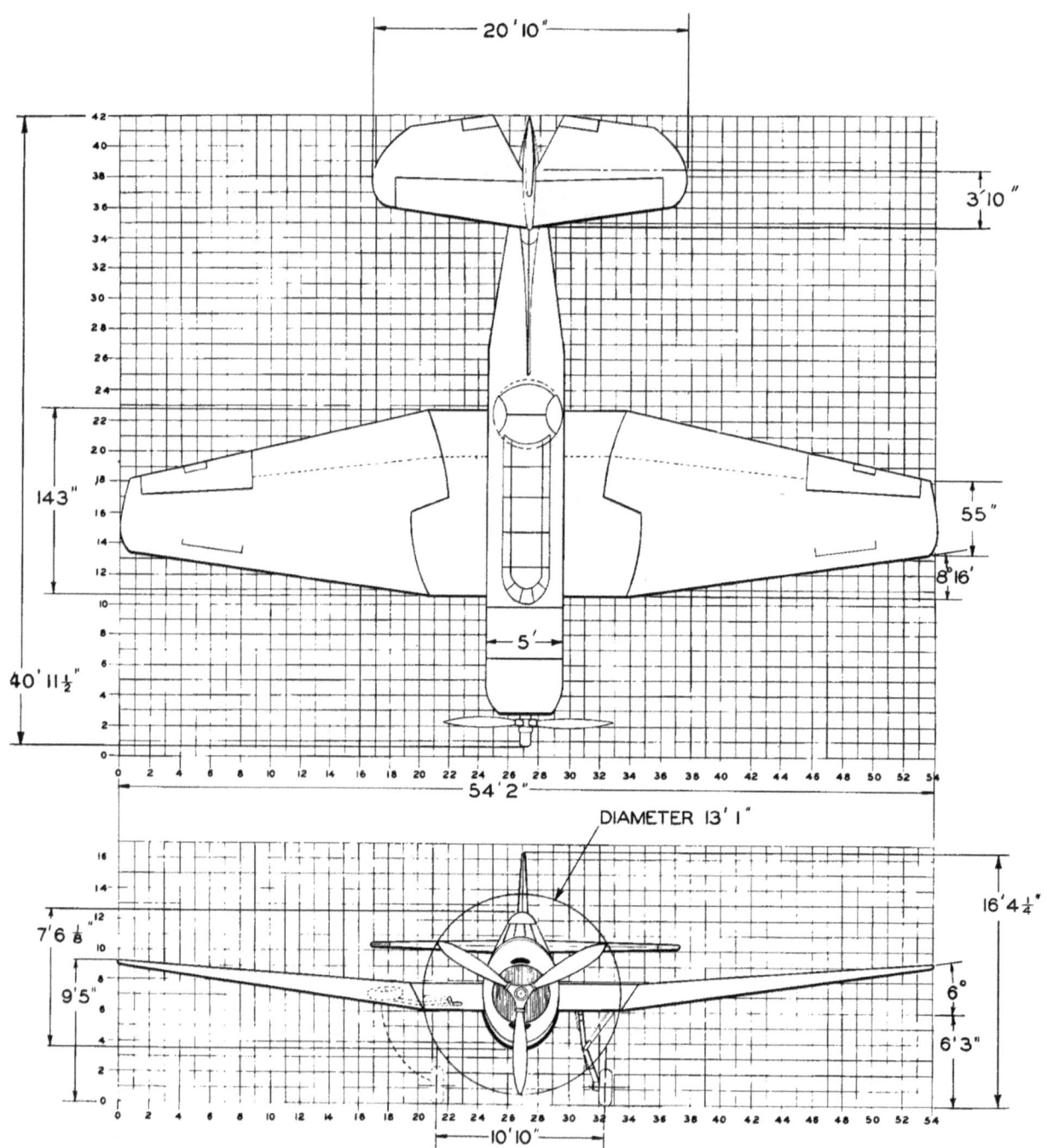

Figure 3 — Principle Dimensions

b. PROTECTION FROM GUNFIRE.—Armor is provided to minimize the possibility of enemy gunfire reaching the pilot (Figure 4A) and turret gunner (Figure 4).

c. HYDRAULIC SYSTEM.

(1) The hydraulic system operates in several different circuits, each of which is supplied hydraulic pressure from a central distributing unit. A separate control is provided for each circuit. The circuits are as follows:

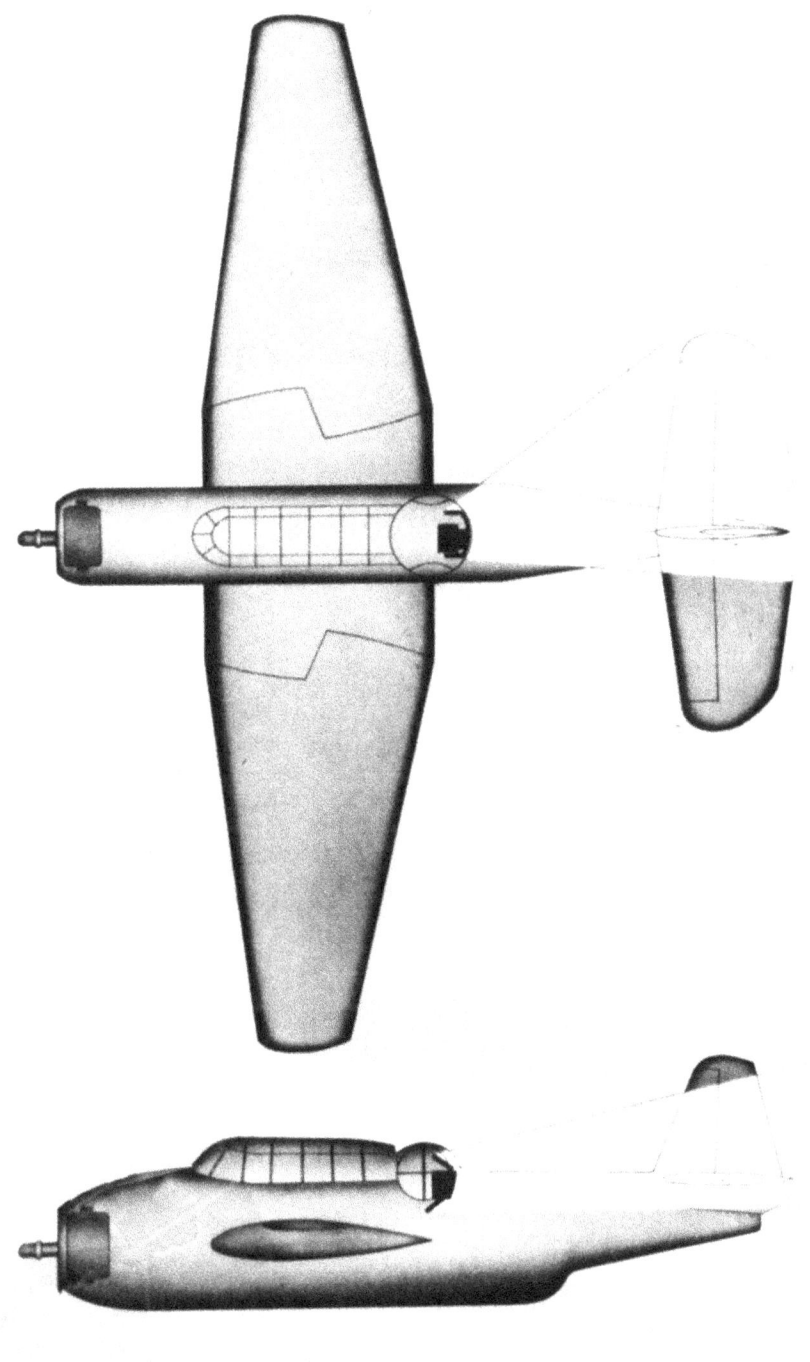

Figure 4 — Protection from Gunfire, Turret Position

Figure 4A — Protection from Gunfire, Pilot's Position

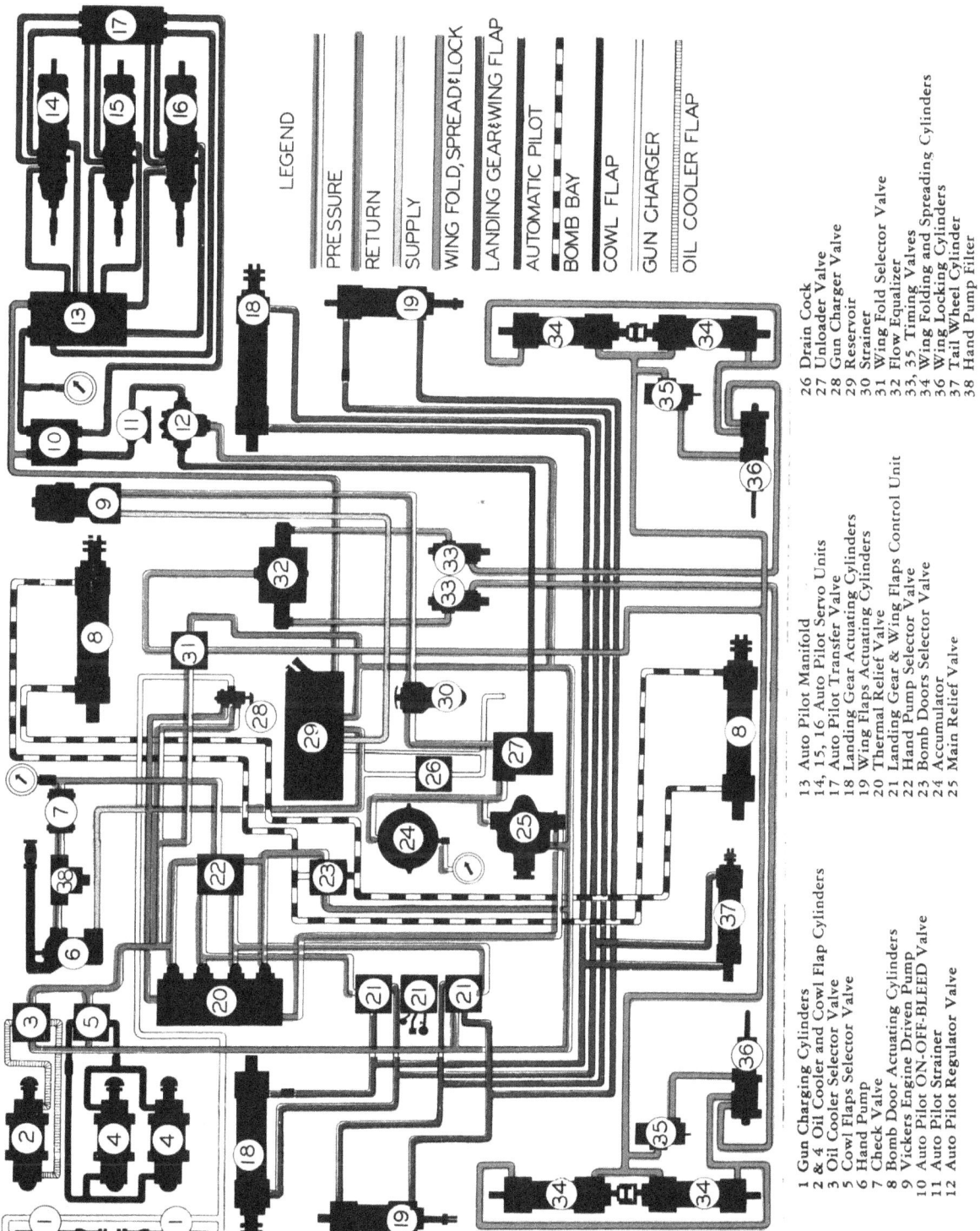

Figure 5 — Hydraulic System, Schematic

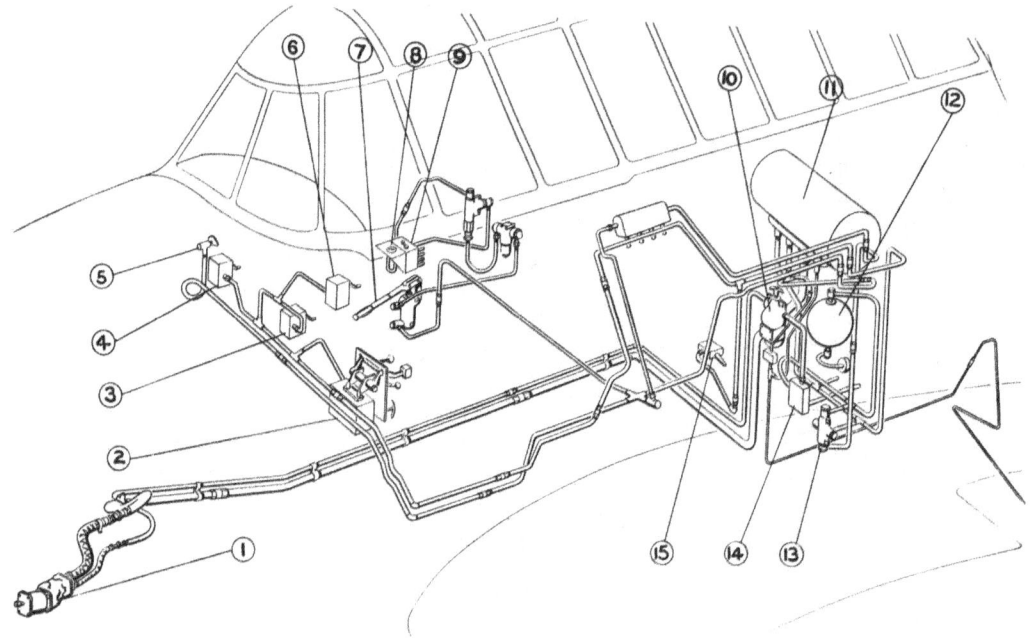

1 Engine Driven Pump
2 Landing Gear and Wing Flap Control Unit
3 Cowl Flap Selector Valve
4 Wing Folding and Spreading Selector Valve
5 Gun Charger Valve
6 Oil Cooler Selector Valve
7 Hand Pump
8 Pressure Gage
9 Hand Pump Selector Valve
10 Filter
11 Reservoir
12 Accumulator
13 Main Pressure Relief Valve
14 Unloader Valve
15 Bomb Bay Door Selector Valve

Figure 6 — Hydraulic System

(a) Landing Gear.
(b) Wing Flaps.
(c) Wing Folding, Spreading and Locking.
(d) Bomb Bay Doors.
(e) Cowl Flaps.
(f) Oil Cooler Flap.
(g) Wing Guns Charger.
(h) Automatic Pilot.

(2) Pressure is generated by an engine-driven pump or by the auxiliary hand pump on the floor of the cockpit, port aft of pilot's seat.

(3) A pressure gage mounted above the hand pump registers the system pressure. The system pressure gage will show a drop in pressure when a circuit is in operation, but will build up again when the circuit is closed, unless there is a leak in the system. The system pressure gage will read between 1250 and 1500 p.s.i. when the hydraulic system is functioning properly.

(4) The distribution unit, located on the vertical bulkhead forward of the bombardier's seat, consists of a Reservoir, Strainer, Unloader Valve, Main Pres-

Figure 7 — Hydraulic Pressure Gage

sure Relief Valve and Accumulator. The pressure regulating unloader valve controls the pressure in the system between 1250 and 1500 p.s.i. When the unloader valve is by-passing hydraulic fluid from the engine driven pump, the fluid flows to the automatic pilot pressure regulator. When any unit in the hydraulic system is being actuated, no fluid will flow to the automatic pilot. The Accumulator acts as a shock absorber in the system and as a small reserve source of pressure sufficient to operate any one circuit.

(5) The Auxiliary Hand Pump is used to supply pressure if the engine is not running, or in case the engine-driven pump fails. It is also used to locate a break in the circuits.

Circuits with broken lines may be isolated by placing the selector valve in the neutral position, which is midway between the ends of the stroke.

CAUTION

When a leak is located, the damaged circuit must not be used. Hydraulic fluid must be conserved for use in the remaining circuits.

(6) The hydraulic fluid used in this system is a mineral oil conforming to Specification AN-VV-O-366, colored "red". No other hydraulic fluid shall be used. The characteristic "red" color helps to locate leaks quickly.

(7) The airplane is equipped with Purolator protected restrictors to filter out impurities in the individual circuits to maintain proper operation.

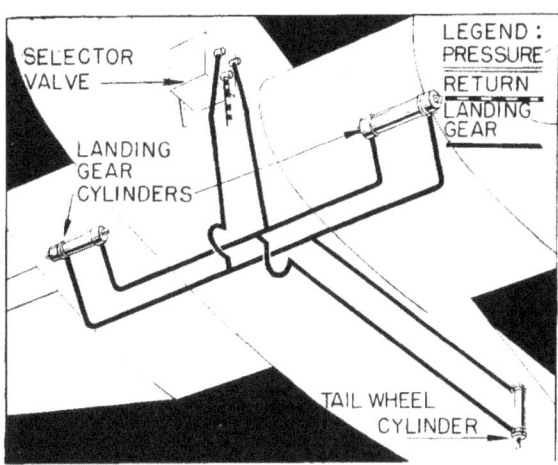

Figure 8 — Landing Gear Hydraulic Circuit

d. ELECTRICAL SYSTEM.

(1) The electrical system is a single wire, ground return type. Current is supplied by an engine-driven generator which carries the load and recharges two 12 volt, 34 ampere-hour batteries connected in series.

(2) A DC receptacle is provided for plugging in a battery cart power plug for engine starting, for operating the turret when the plane is grounded, or for checking the electrical system. This receptacle is on the lower right side of the fuselage. Adjacent to it is an AC power receptacle for ground checking special radio devices.

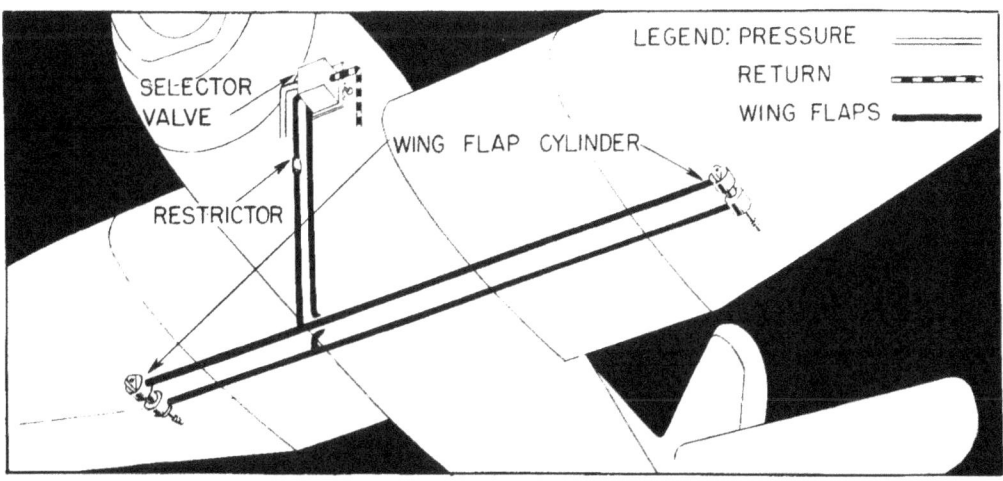

Figure 9 — Wing Flap Hydraulic Circuit

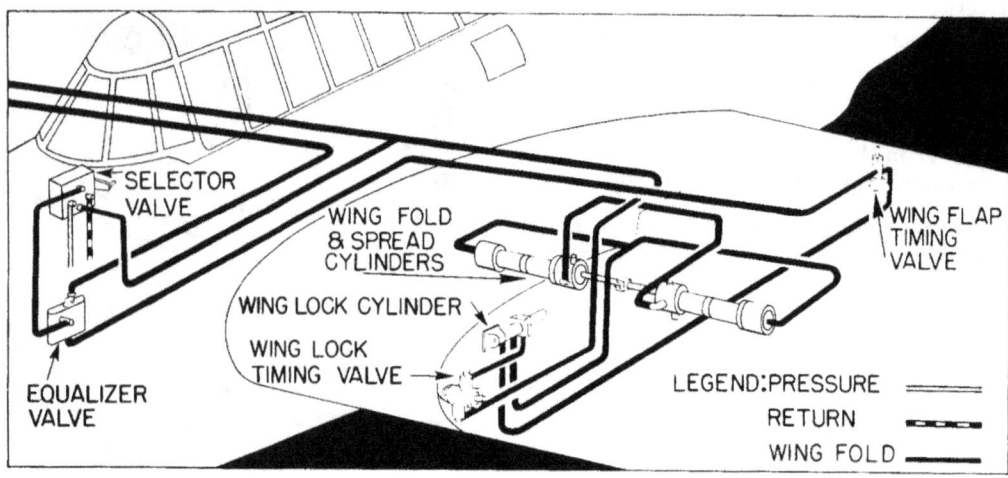

Figure 10 — Wing Fold, Spread and Lock Hydraulic Circuit

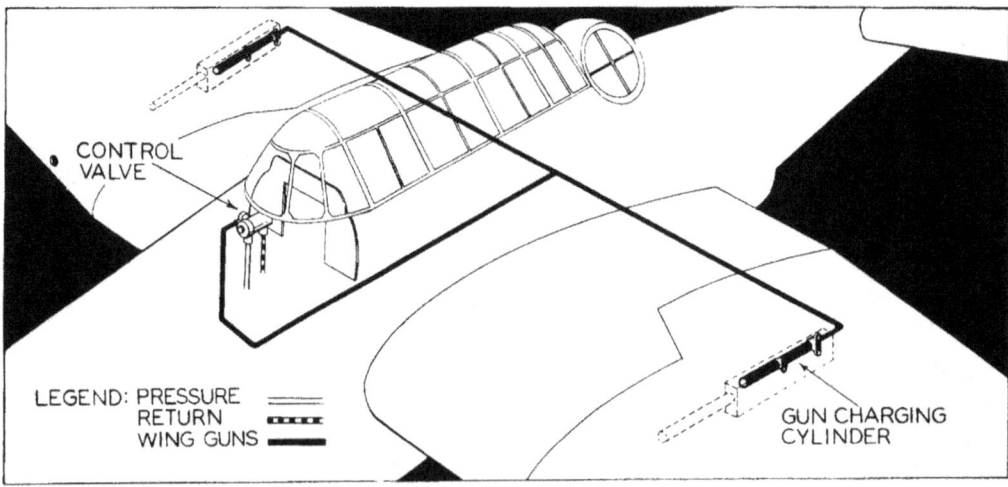

Figure 11 — Wing Gun Charger Hydraulic Circuit

(3) The battery switch must be ON to operate any of the electric units, with the exception of the recognition lights and IFF inertia switch circuit, which are connected directly to the battery. The battery voltage can be read on the voltmeter when the battery switch is ON.

(4) When opening and closing any switch, especially the battery switch, use a fast positive action to minimize arcing and burning of contact points.

(5) Before turning the battery switch on or off, check to make sure that all transmitter switches and the turret power switch are turned OFF.

(6) There are containers for spare bulbs in the pilot's cockpit and in the bombardier's compartment. A complete wiring diagram is in the pocket on the left side of the cockpit.

WARNING

Regard electrical apparatus generally, and especially all current-carrying parts, as dangerous irrespective of voltage. Exercise great care in handling, and avoid broad contacts such as are made by standing on a metal deck or in water.

2. POWER PLANT

a. ENGINE.

(1) GENERAL.—The airplane is powered by the Wright-Cyclone 14 Aircraft Engine Series C14-BB Model R-2600-20, manufactured by the Wright Aeronautical Corporation. The engine is a 14-cylinder, staggered two row radial air cooled type. The propeller is driven at a ratio of 16 to 9 crankshaft speed by means of reduction gears. The supercharger is of the two speed, single stage, centrifugal type, having an impeller which is driven at a ratio of 7.06 to 1 when operating in LOW blower, and a ratio of 10.06 to 1 crankshaft speed when operating in HIGH blower. The carburetor is a model PR48-A3 Stromberg injection carburetor, incorporating automatic altitude mixture control and idle cut-off.

(2) MILITARY POWER.—The engine is designed to operate for periods up to five minutes only at this power, provided temperature limits are not exceeded.

b. PROPELLER.—The propeller is a three blade, Hamilton-Standard Hydromatic with a constant speed control. There is a manual selection control on the upper left section of the pilot's instrument panel (see Figure 27).

c. OIL SYSTEM. (Fig. 12)

(1) OIL.—Use oil in accordance with AN Spec. AN-VV-O-446.

(2) The oil tank is forward of the fire-wall in the engine accessory compartment. The normal amount of oil in the tank and lines is approximately 13 gallons. The maximum oil capacity is approximately 32 gallons. There is a sounding rod located near the filler neck to determine the quantity in the tank when the plane is in normal ground position.

(3) The actual quantity of oil carried will depend upon the oil consumption of the engine and the type of operation or mission. As a general rule, a fuel-oil ratio of 15/1 will be satisfactory. This ratio should be varied to about 18/1 for long range cruising power operation; for operations involving especially severe scavenging and foaming conditions, such as continued carrier landing practice, it is advisable to carry not less than 20 nor more than 25 gallons of oil.

(4) The scavenged oil passes through an oil cooler, equipped with a fully automatic temperature regulator incorporating a by-pass valve, which directs the oil flow either through the core of the oil cooler or through the by-pass to the oil supply tank.

A hydraulically operated cooler flap, below the engine compartment, permits control of air through the oil cooler. The selector valve for the oil cooler flap is located on the pilot's lower port instrument panel (see Figure 26).

(5) An oil dilution system is provided to facilitate starting on some of the TBM-3 airplanes. This system is used before stopping the engine when a cold weather start is anticipated. Dilution is obtained by the addition of engine fuel into the oil inlet line at the base of the oil tank and is controlled by a toggle switch in the cockpit (see Figure 47).

d. FUEL SYSTEM. (Fig. 13).

(1) Use grade 100/130 fuel in accordance with AN Specification AN-F-28.

(2) The fuel is carried in the wing center section in three tanks equipped with self-sealing liners. A droppable fuel tank can be carried in the bomb-bay and under each wing.

(3) The maximum capacity of the tanks is indicated on their respective filler caps and is approximately as follows:

Tank	U. S. gallons	British Imp. gallons
Center Main	145	121
Left Main	90	75
Right Main	90	75
Bomb Bay non-droppable (Self-Sealing)	212	176.6
Bomb Bay Droppable	270	225
Droppable Left Wing	58 or 100	48.3 or 83.3
Droppable Right Wing	58 or 100	48.3 or 83.3

These quantities do not allow for expansion space.

(4) The tank filler caps are located as follows:

Right Main — Right Walkway
Left Main — Left Walkway
Center Main—Left side of Fuselage
Droppable — Right wing outboard of Walkway

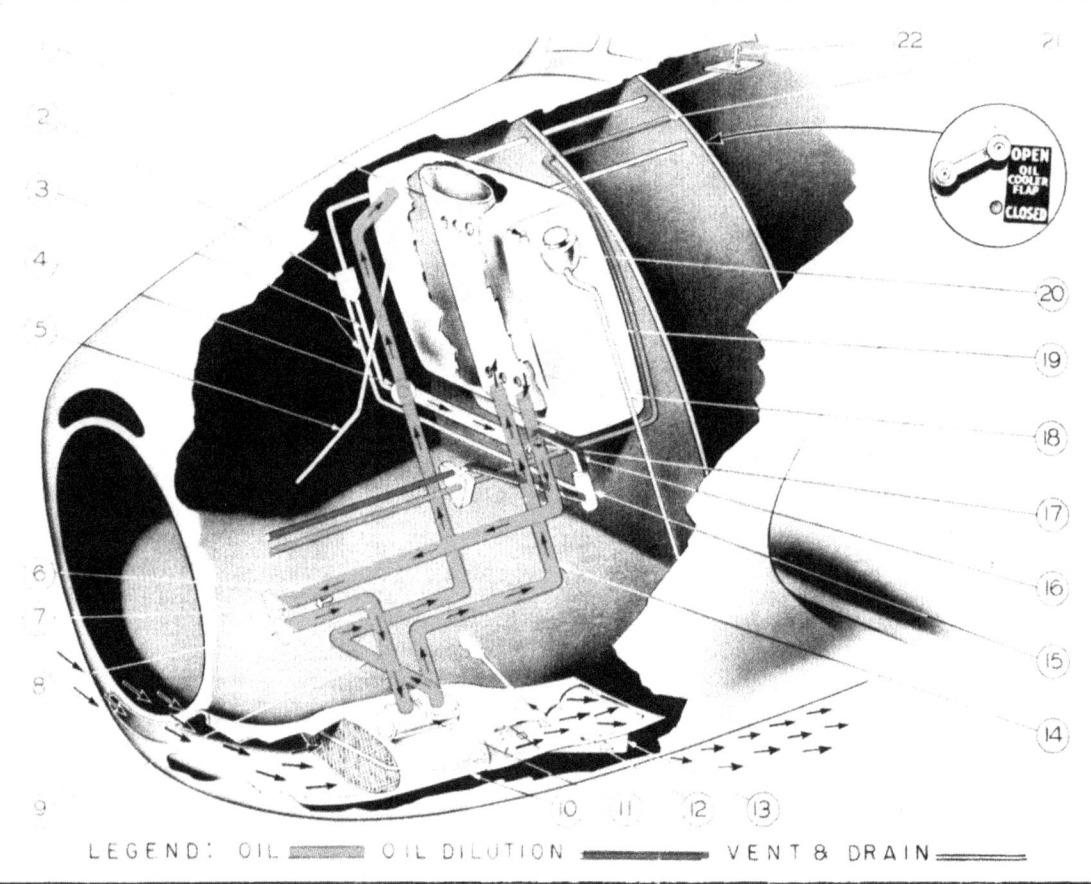

1 Sounding Rod.
2 Engine Junction Box.
3 Lines Operating Oil Dilution System.
4 Oil Diverter Valve.
5 Vent Line from Crank Case to Top of Tank.
6 Oil Line from Tank to Engine.
7 Drain Valve.
8 Oil Line from Engine to Regulator.
9 Oil Line from Oil Cooler to Diverter Valve.
10 Oil Cooler.
11 Oil Regulator.
12 Hydraulic Cylinder and Rod for Operating Cooler Flap.
13 Oil Cooler Flap.
14 Oil Line from Oil Regulator to Tank.
15 Electrical Oil Dilution Valve.
16 Oil Dilution Line.
17 Manual Oil Dilution Valve.
18 Overflow Pan Drain.
19 Oil Tank.
20 Filler Unit & Strainer.
21 Oil Pressure Line.
22 Oil Dilution Control.

Figure 12 — Oil System

Section I

AN 01-190EB-1

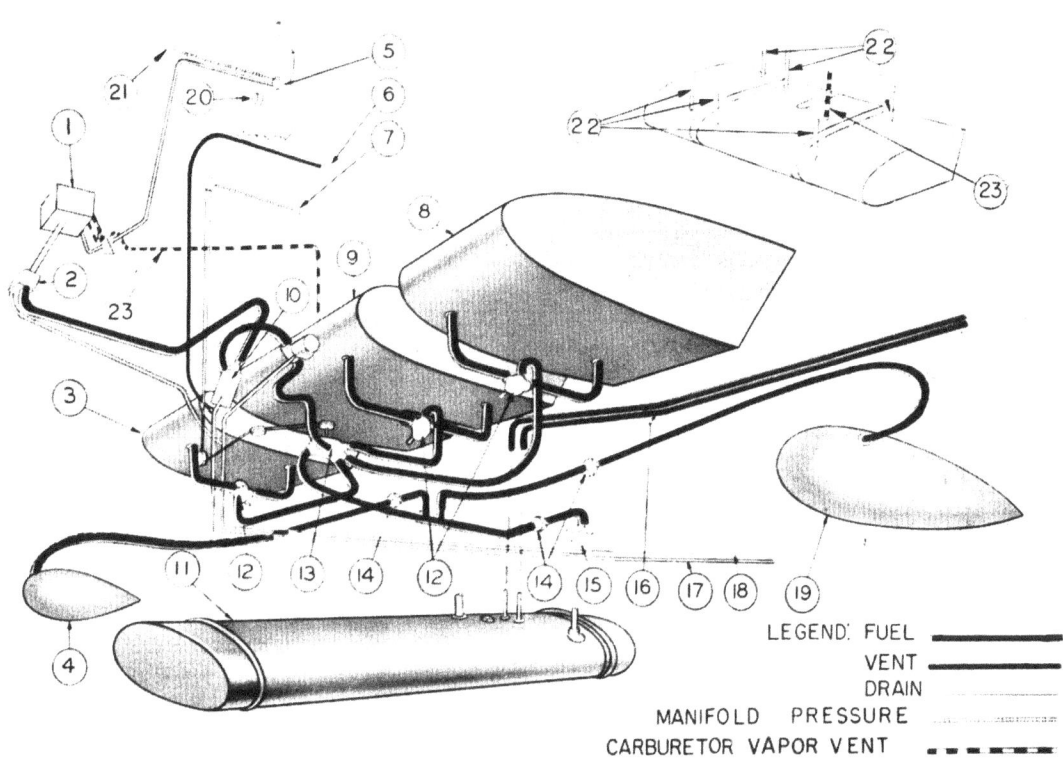

1. Carburetor
2. Fuel Pump
3. Right Main Fuel Tank
4. Right Wing Droppable Fuel Tank
5. Fuel Pressure Gage
6. Fuel Strainer Drain Control
7. Fuel Tank Selector Valve Control
8. Left Main Fuel Tank
9. Center Main Fuel Tank
10. Main Fuel Strainer & Drain
11. Bomb Bay Fuel Tank
12. Main Tank Sumps and Drains
13. Fuel Tank Selector Valve
14. Electric ON and OFF Switches for Droppable Fuel Tanks
17. Main Strainer Drain Line
18. Fuel Pump Drain Line
19. Left Wing Droppable Fuel Tank
20. Dual Vapor Vent Line
21. Manifold Pressure Line
22. Vent Lines
23. Carburetor Vapor Vent Return Line

Figure 13 — Fuel System

(5) The center droppable tank, when used, is suspended in the bomb bay and the droppable wing tanks, when used, are suspended one under each wing, just inboard of the wing folding axis. Fuel from each of the three droppable tanks is piped into a single junction, which runs to the inlet port of the fuel tank selector valve. Before the junction point of each of these lines, electrically operated valves are installed with ON-OFF switches for individual selection of left, center, or right droppable tanks. When any one of these tanks has served its purpose it may be dropped in flight.

(6) A Fuel Strainer is provided to permit daily draining of any impurities which may accumulate in the fuel system. Drain control is located on the pilot's sub panel above the port rudder pedal (see Figure 38).

(7) The fuel is normally delivered by the engine driven pump, but an electrically driven auxiliary pump is provided to build up initial pressure for starting the engine, to maintain fuel pressure at high altitude, for emergency use in case of engine driven fuel pump failure, for take-off, landing and to maintain fuel pressure while switching from one tank to another.

3. CONTROLS.

a. AIRPLANE CONTROLS.

(1) AILERON AND ELEVATOR.—A conventional stick, equipped with pistol type grip, is provided. To lock controls, place the metal cap over the control stick, hook the two attached wire cables into the rudder pedals and attach the elastic cords by means of hooks to the bulkhead immediately behind the pilot's seat as shown in figure 14.

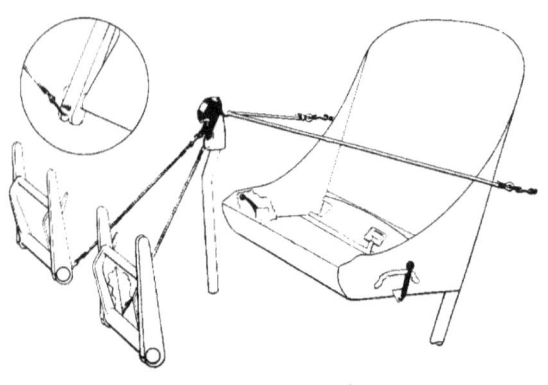

Figure 14 — Stick and Harness

(2) RUDDER AND BRAKE CONTROL.—The rudder pedals are of the standard underhung type, adjustable to three positions for different leg lengths. The adjustment levers are located on the arm on the inboard side of each pedal. With toes on adjustment levers, push pedals forward as far as possible, then with toes under the pedals pull them AFT one notch at a time, until the desired position is reached. Make sure that each pedal has ratcheted past the same number of notches. Power for the hydraulic brakes is supplied by cylinders attached to the pedals. The braking elements in the wheels are alternate rotating and stationary discs, which are pressed together when the pilot pushes on the forward edges (the upper part) of the pedals.

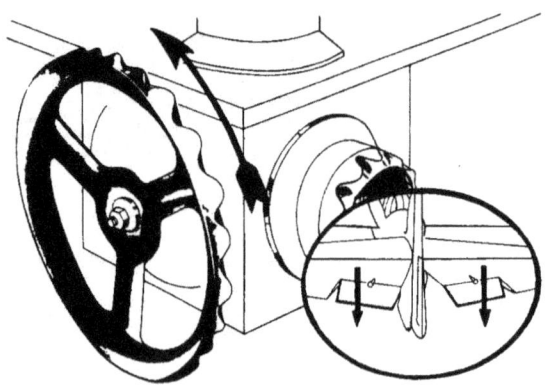

Figure 15 — Elevator Trim Tab Control

(3) ELEVATOR TRIM TAB CONTROL.—The elevator tab control handwheel, on the inboard face of the trim tab control unit, at the left of the pilot's seat, adjusts the longitudinal trim of the airplane. To trim the airplane turn the handwheel in the direction of action required, COUNTERCLOCKWISE will raise the nose, CLOCKWISE will lower the nose.

(4) RUDDER TRIM TAB CONTROL.—The rudder trim tab knob, on the top of the control unit at the left of the pilot's seat, adjusts the directional trim of the airplane. Turn the knob in the direction of the desired resultant motion of the airplane; CLOCKWISE to turn nose right, COUNTERCLOCKWISE to turn nose left.

(5) AILERON TRIM TAB CONTROL.—The aileron trim tab control, on the forward end of the control unit, adjusts the lateral trim of the airplane.

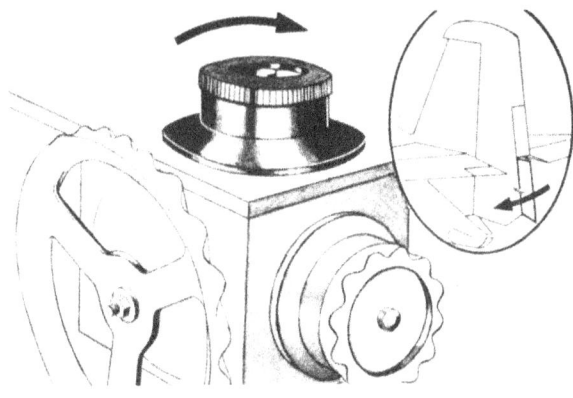

Figure 16 — Rudder Trim Tab Control

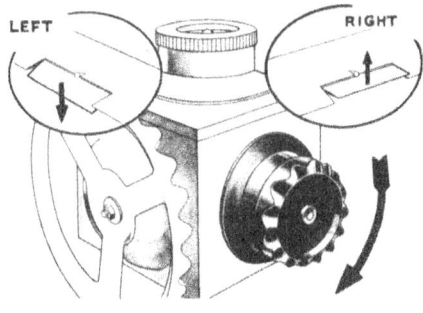

Figure 17 — Aileron Trim Tab Control

Turn the knob in the direction of the desired resultant motion of the airplane; CLOCKWISE to raise the starboard wing, COUNTERCLOCKWISE to raise the port wing.

b. POWER PLANT CONTROLS.

(1) FUEL STRAINER DRAIN.—The fuel strainer should be drained daily just prior to flight. It is controlled by a push-pull knob on the panel above the port rudder pedal. Press center of knob to unlock, then pull OUT to drain strainer, hold for approximately five seconds, then push FULL IN. Be sure to leave closed after draining.

(2) QUANTITY GAGES.—There are four electrically operated fuel quantity gages in one unit, located on the lower starboard side of the instrument panel. These gages indicate the fuel quantity of the three main tanks and the center auxiliary tank. No provision is made to indicate the fuel in the wing droppable tanks.

(3) FUEL TANK SELECTOR.—This control is located on the panel, directly forward of the stick. It has five positions marked on its dial, which are:

Off	Right Main
Center Main	Droppable
Left Main	

To change tanks, turn the selector handle to the tank desired making sure that it is turned far enough so that it is felt to seat. The auxiliary fuel pumps should be turned ON while shifting tanks.

(4) AUXILIARY FUEL PUMP.—The auxiliary fuel pump is controlled by a toggle switch near the tab controls on the pilot's port side. The pump is used to build up pressure for starting the engine, to maintain fuel pressure at high altitudes, for emergency use in case of engine driven fuel pump failure and to maintain fuel pressure while changing tanks. This pump is turned ON for take-off and landing as an added precaution to maintain an adequate steady fuel pressure.

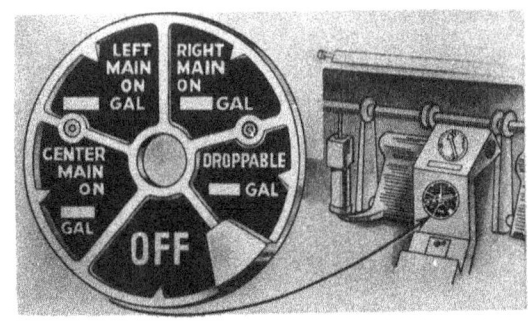

Figure 18 — Fuel Tank Selector

(5) ENGINE CONTROL QUADRANT.—This is located on the left side of the pilot's cockpit. It contains the following:

(*a*) THROTTLE CONTROL.—
Lever Aft—CLOSED.
Lever Forward—OPEN.

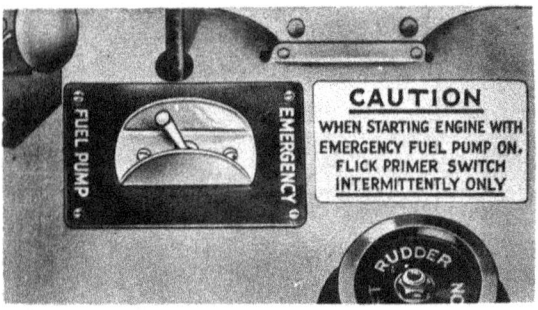

Figure 19 — Auxiliary Fuel Pump Switch

(b) MIXTURE CONTROL.—
Idle Cut Off—Lever Aft (Red Sector).
Automatic Lean—Lever Center (AL White Sector).
Automatic Rich—Lever Full Forward (AR White Sector).

Fuel will flow through the carburetor with the mixture control in any position except cut-off, whenever the fuel pressure is greater than five p.s.i., whether the engine is running or stopped. The mixture control should therefore be left in the cut-off position whenever the engine is not running to prevent fuel from collecting in the supercharger. If for any reason during ground operations the engine should cut out, the mixture control should be immediately moved to the cut-off position to prevent flooding the fuel induction system.

Figure 20 — Engine Control Quadrant

(c) SUPERCHARGER CONTROL.—
Full Forward—LOW BLOWER.
Full Aft—HIGH BLOWER.

(d) FRICTION ADJUSTMENT.—Rotate knob on side of quadrant clockwise to increase friction.

(6) CARBURETOR AIR CONTROL.—A push-pull "T" handle, on the upper left side of the main instrument panel is used to operate the deflector door in the carburetor air intake. In the DIRECT (in) position, outside air goes directly to the carburetor and in the ALTERNATE (out) position, it must pass by the engine cylinders. Lift the handle to unlock.

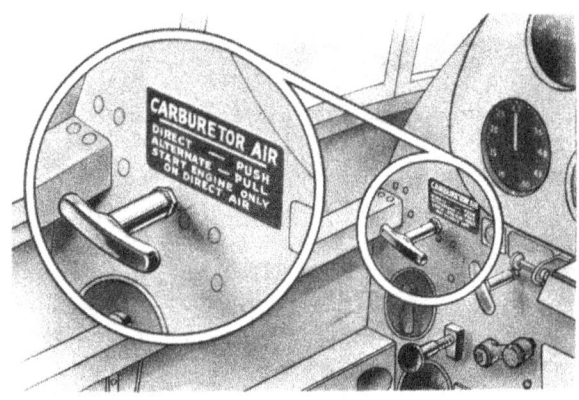

Figure 21 — Carburetor Air Control

(7) COWL FLAPS CONTROL.—The cowl flaps are controlled by a three position hydraulic control lever located directly above the left rudder pedal.

LEVER UP—FLAPS OPEN

LEVER CENTER—NEUTRAL.

LEVER DOWN—FLAPS CLOSED.

Cowl flaps must be FULL OPEN for all ground operation to avoid "cooking" the electrical harness. This applies to warm-ups in cold weather as well as warm weather. At normal temperatures, all level flight and cruising climbs can be done with closed cowl flaps. When leveling off for cruising, best results will be obtained by leaving the cowl flaps partly open until the head temperature drops to 190° C (374° F), and then closing the cowl flaps, after which a rise to 218° C (424° F), is permissible. The flaps may be stopped in any intermediate position by returning the control to NEUTRAL.

Figure 22 — Cowl Flaps Control

Note

Cowl flap drag when in OPEN position is in excess of 20 knots (24 mph) at maximum velocity; keep closed when temperatures permit.

(8) IGNITION SWITCH.—This switch is located on the left side of the instrument panel. It has four positions:

Both magnetos off—OFF.

Right magneto on—R.

Left magneto on—L.

Both magnetos on—BOTH.

(9) THE STARTER.—

(*a*) ELECTRICAL OPERATION.—The starter switch is located on the distribution panel. The booster coil is energized only when the starter switch is held in the mesh position.

Figure 24 — Starter Switch

Left—Starter (not over 15 seconds).
Right—Mesh.

An external electrical source should be used if available.

Note

If the starter does not energize, move switch to mesh momentarily to insure that the brushes which might have been lifted and locked for hand cranking are released and back on the commutator.

(*b*) MANUAL OPERATION OF STARTER.— The gear box and handle are stowed in the bombardier's compartment below the door. In manual operation of the starter the gear box and handle must be meshed with the starter cable located at the lower starboard side of the fuselage just forward of the bomb bay doors. Pull engaging cable "T" handle control full out and allow to snap back, this lifts and locks the brushes. Turn starter handcrank until sufficient speed is obtained, then pull engaging cable "T" handle once more to start the engine.

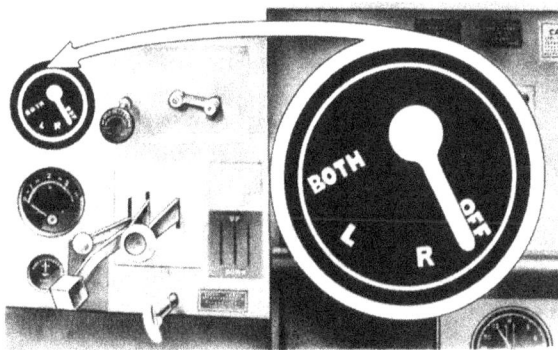

Figure 23 — Ignition Switch

Figure 25 — Starter Crank

Figure 26 — Oil Cooler Flap Control

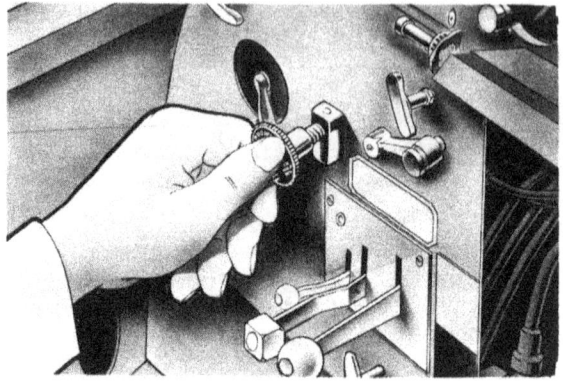

Figure 27 — Propeller Control

(10) ELECTRIC PRIMER.—The primer is operated by a toggle switch on the pilot's distribution panel.

(11) OIL COOLER FLAP CONTROL.—The oil cooler flap is controlled by a two position hydraulic control lever, located on the left side of the main instrument panel.

    LEVER UP—FLAP OPEN.
    LEVER DOWN—FLAP CLOSED.

The flap can be operated by the hydraulic hand pump in conjunction with the Hand Pump Selector Valve Control.

(12) PROPELLER CONTROL.—The propeller governor is controlled by a push-pull knob, located on the left side of the main instrument panel.

    Push In—INCREASE RPM (DECREASE PITCH).

    Pull Out—DECREASE RPM (INCREASE PITCH).

For vernier control, turn control knob clockwise to increase RPM and counterclockwise to decrease RPM.

The operating range of the constant speed governor unit is from 1200 RPM to 2800 RPM. Within this range, the engine RPM should be regulated entirely by the propeller governor control, the throttle being used to regulate the manifold pressure. Once so selected, the RPM will remain constant under all conditions, within the operating limits of the governor.

Always move the push-pull control knob slowly. Slight movement makes a great change in RPM.

(13) ELECTRIC SWITCHES FOR DROPPABLE TANKS.—An electric "ON-OFF" switch for each of the droppable tanks to be used in conjunction with the tank selector valve is located below the tank selector valve.

(14) DROPPABLE TANK RELEASES.—The center droppable tank can be dropped after it has served its purpose by opening the bomb bay doors and pulling emergency bomb release "T" handle. It cannot be released electrically.

The wing droppable tanks can be released manually by the pilot. The two chrome yellow "T" handles directly below the chart board are for this purpose. Pull the one on the left to release the tank below the left wing section and the one on the right to release the tank below the right wing section.

c. ALIGHTING GEAR.

(1) CONTROLS.

(*a*) The hydraulic control unit on the lower left side of the instrument panel combines the control of the alighting gear and the wing flaps. To raise or lower the wheels, move the lever with the large square knob to the desired position, as indicated:

LEVER UP—WHEELS RETRACTED (UP)
    TIME REQUIRED—15 sec. (approx.).
LEVER DOWN—WHEELS EXTENDED (DOWN)
    TIME REQUIRED—12 sec. (approx.).

WARNING

THERE IS NO INTERCONNECTION BETWEEN WING FLAP AND LANDING GEAR LEVERS IN ALL CURRENT AIRPLANES. IT IS NECESSARY TO MOVE LANDING GEAR LEVER SEPARATELY TO RAISE OR LOWER LANDING GEAR. HOWEVER, ON AIRPLANES UNMODIFIED IN SERVICE, THERE IS AN INTERLOCK.

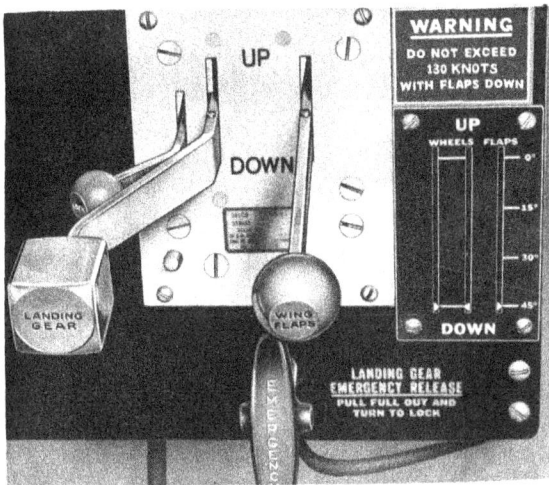

Figure 28 — Alighting Gear and Wing Flap Control

(b) Airplanes not modified in Service to remove interlock between the wing flap and landing gear controls are identified by the presence of the release lever on the wing flap control handle and do not incorporate a clip riveted to the wing flap control handle to hold the release lever open. Moving the wing flap lever to the DOWN position also lowers the wheels, unless the release lever on the wing flap control is depressed.

(c) Model TBM-3 Airplanes, Serial Nos. 23634 and subsequent have been modified in production to remove the interlock between wing flap and landing gear controls. *On these airplanes the auxiliary LOCK lever must be raised to retract the landing gear, regardless of flap setting.* These airplanes may be identified by the landing gear control handle which is painted YELLOW.

(d) Model TBM-3 Airplanes previous to Serial No. 23634 may be modified one of several ways, as follows:

1. Airplanes, Serial Nos. 23457 through 23633, were modified on a quick fix basis prior to delivery to remove the release lever on the wing flap control or to incorporate a clip riveted to the wing flap control handle to hold the release lever open.

2. Airplanes, Serial Nos. previous to 23457, were modified in Service to incorporate a clip riveted to the wing flap control handle to hold the release lever open.

3. Airplanes, Serial Nos. previous to 23457, not yet modified in Service to remove the interlock between wing flap and landing gear controls. *On all airplanes previous to Serial No. 23634 the auxiliary LOCK lever must be raised to retract the landing gear with flaps DOWN but need not be raised with flaps UP.* These airplanes do not have landing gear control handle painted YELLOW.

(e) The landing gear shall not be lowered at speeds in excess of 200 knots (230 mph) and shall not be retracted at speeds in excess of 150 knots (173 mph).

(f) If pressure in the hydraulic system is being supplied by the hand pump, the hand pump selector valve should be in the position marked LANDING GEAR.

(g) In the event of complete failure of the hydraulic system, the wheels can be lowered by pulling the landing gear emergency release "T" handle, located directly below the hydraulic control. Reduce airspeed to 95 knots (110 mph) or less before pulling the emergency release handle. Lock it by rotating it 45 degrees clockwise. The weight of the wheels and the action of the springs in the actuating cylinders should cause the wheels to drop and lock in the full down position.

CAUTION

Before pulling the emergency release handle, move the hydraulic control lever to the "UP" position to lift the landing gear off the hooks. Leave in the UP position while pulling the emergency release, then return to the DOWN position.

(h) If the emergency release does not release the landing gear it may be released from the up-locks by applying a negative gravity maneuver and pulling the emergency release handle.

(i) After landing investigate the cause for the hydraulic failure, restore normal operation of the hydraulic system and return the emergency release handle to its normal position.

(j) A mechanical indicator is provided to show the pilot the position of the main wheels. The two points in the slots to the right of the levers show UP or DOWN for each wheel.

(2) MAIN WHEEL LOCKS.

(a) A mechanical connection between the alighting gear control lever and the left shock strut holds the lever in the DOWN position when the airplane is on the ground. The lever can be moved to the UP position only in flight, when the struts are fully extended.

(b) On the ground, mechanically operated locks prevent the side struts from breaking under a load. In flight, when the wheels are being retracted, the hydraulic cylinders release this lock before the lifting action starts.

(c) In the UP position, the main wheels are locked by hooks that snap onto bars attached to the shock struts. These locks are released by mechanical action when the control lever is set to DOWN or when the emergency "T" handle is pulled.

(3) TAIL WHEEL CASTER LOCK.—The tail wheel caster lock control lever is located on the port side. It is operated as follows:

(*a*) SHORE BASE.—The tail wheel caster lock must be LOCKED during take-off and landing to reduce the possibility of ground looping. LOCK immediately after taxiing into position for take-off. UNLOCK after completing the landing run.

(*b*) CARRIER BASE.—The tail wheel caster lock must be LOCKED for take-off and must be LOCKED until the landing gear is fully lowered in landing approach. UNLOCK before landing.

WARNING

The tail wheel caster lock must be LOCKED until the landing gear has been fully lowered in carrier landing approach to prevent the possibility of the tail wheel sticking in the wheel well during the lowering operation.

(4) OPERATION CHECK.—Before lowering the wheels, reduce the air speed to less than 200 knots (230 mph). Then check the pressure in the hydraulic system. If it is less than 1150 p.s.i. use the hand pump to build it up to 1750 p.s.i. Be sure the hand pump selector valve is set in the LANDING GEAR position. After moving the alighting gear control lever to the DOWN position, and with the arrow-shaped pointers indicating that the wheels are extended, again check the system pressure. If the gauge shows no pressure, pull the emergency "T" handle. This is to insure that the tail wheel has come down.

(5) WARNING SIGNAL.—An electrically operated warning horn is located in the bulkhead just aft of the pilot. This horn will emit a steady warning as soon as the throttle has been adjusted to give a manifold pressure of 15 inches or less unless the landing gear is locked in its full DOWN position ready for landing. An intermittent signal will be heard when any attempt is made to lower the landing gear while the armament master switch is closed and the various armament circuits are operable. This armament warning circuit is not installed on early model TBM-3 airplanes.

The warning horn emits a steady warning signal during wing folding and spreading operations (see Paragraph 3, *e.* (2)).

(6) ARRESTING HOOK CONTROL.—The Arresting Hook is normally operated by a motor which is controlled by a switch and circuit reset button, located at the left of the pilot's seat. An emergency control "T" handle is located on the panel directly

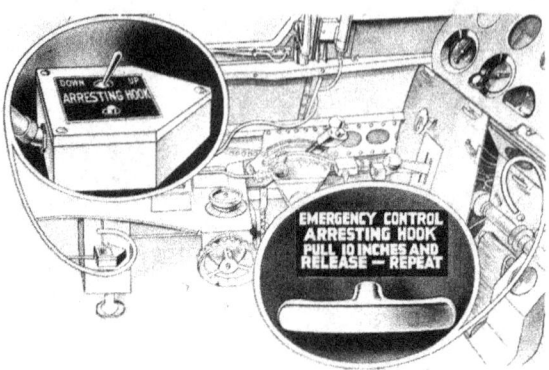

Figure 29 — Arresting Hook Switch and Emergency Control Handle, Internal Arresting Gear

above the port rudder pedal. This handle is used only for extending the hook. To operate, pull the handle out 10 inches and release; repeat 5 or 6 times. If the hook is already extended, this handle cannot be pulled through a full stroke. Before landing aboard a carrier, check to see that the switch is set to the DOWN position and that the manual control cannot be pulled through a full stroke.

Airplanes Navy Serial No. 85566 and subsequent are equipped with an external Arresting Hook. To operate, pull the arresting hook handle and release. (See Figure 29A). Once the Arresting Hook is lowered, it cannot be retracted by the pilot, but must be replaced in its retracted position by the deck crew.

d. WING FLAPS.

(1) The wing flaps are operated by operating the lever with the round knob, placed just to the right of the square knobbed lever on the landing gear and wing flap control unit.

WARNING

THERE IS NO INTERCONNECTION BETWEEN THE WING FLAPS AND LANDING GEAR LEVERS IN ALL CURRENT AIRPLANES. IT IS NECESSARY TO MOVE EACH LEVER UP OR DOWN SEPARATELY, AS CONDITIONS MAY DEMAND, TO RAISE OR LOWER THE LANDING GEAR AND WING FLAPS. HOWEVER, ON AIRPLANES UNMODIFIED IN SERVICE, THERE IS AN INTERLOCK. (SEE PARAGRAPH 3c, ALIGHTING GEAR, FOR IDENTIFICATION.)

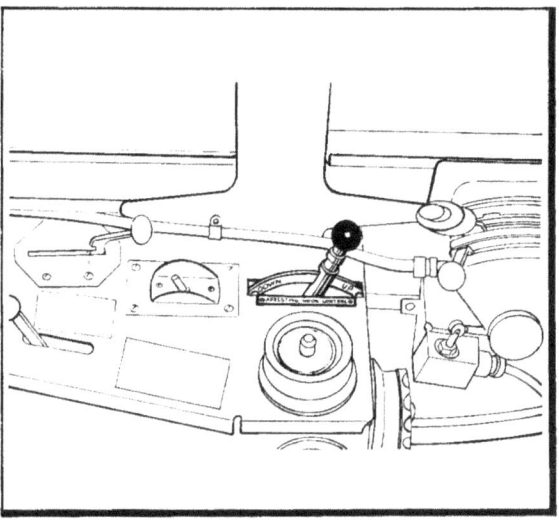

Figure 29A — External Arresting Hook Control Handle

(2) The original unmodified type incorporates an interconnection between the landing gear and wing flaps levers. Lowering the wing flaps will automatically lower the landing gear unless the release lever on the wing flaps lever is depressed. If it is desired to operate the wheels and flaps independently, it is necessary to unlock these controls.

WARNING

PILOT SHOULD MAKE CERTAIN WHAT TYPE CONTROL UNIT IS PRESENT IN AIRPLANE.

(3) If a partial flap setting is used for take-off, with the original unmodified control unit, care must be used in raising the landing gear. To prevent the wing flap control lever from moving up with the landing gear lever, perform the following operations in the sequence given:

(*a*) Move the wing flap control lever (round knob) to the full DOWN position.

(*b*) Raise auxiliary lock lever.

(*c*) Raise landing gear lever (Square knob).

(*d*) Adjust flaps to the desired position.

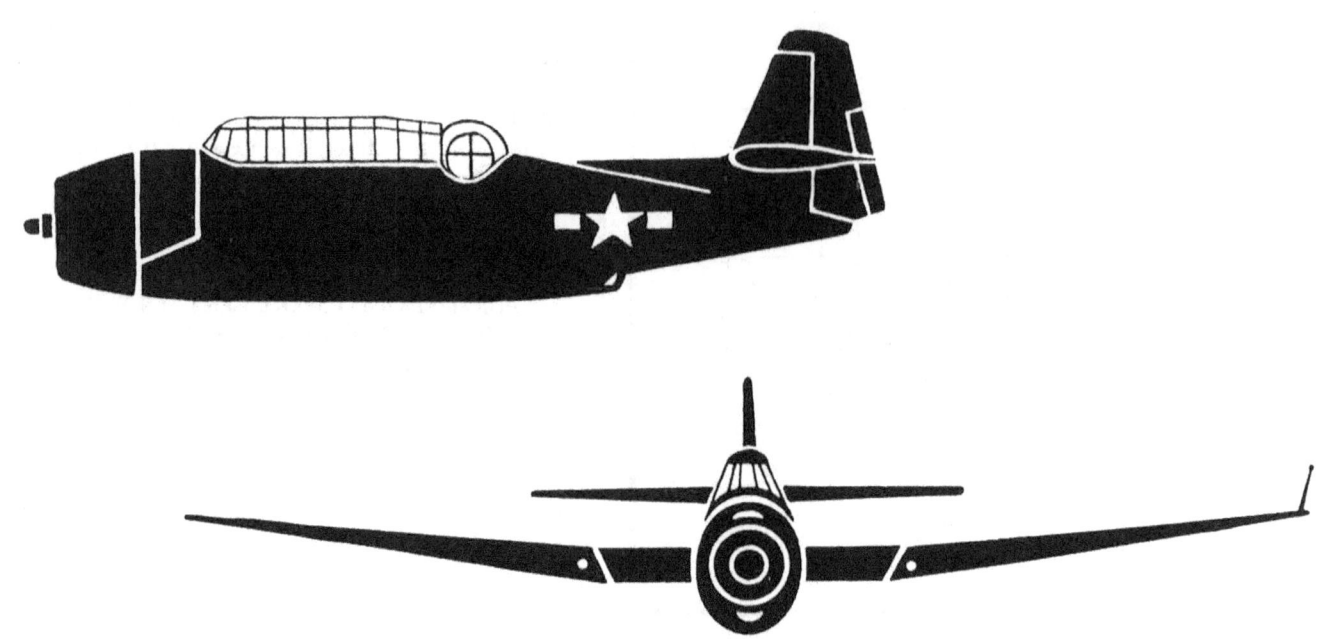

THIS PAGE INTENTIONALLY LEFT BLANK.

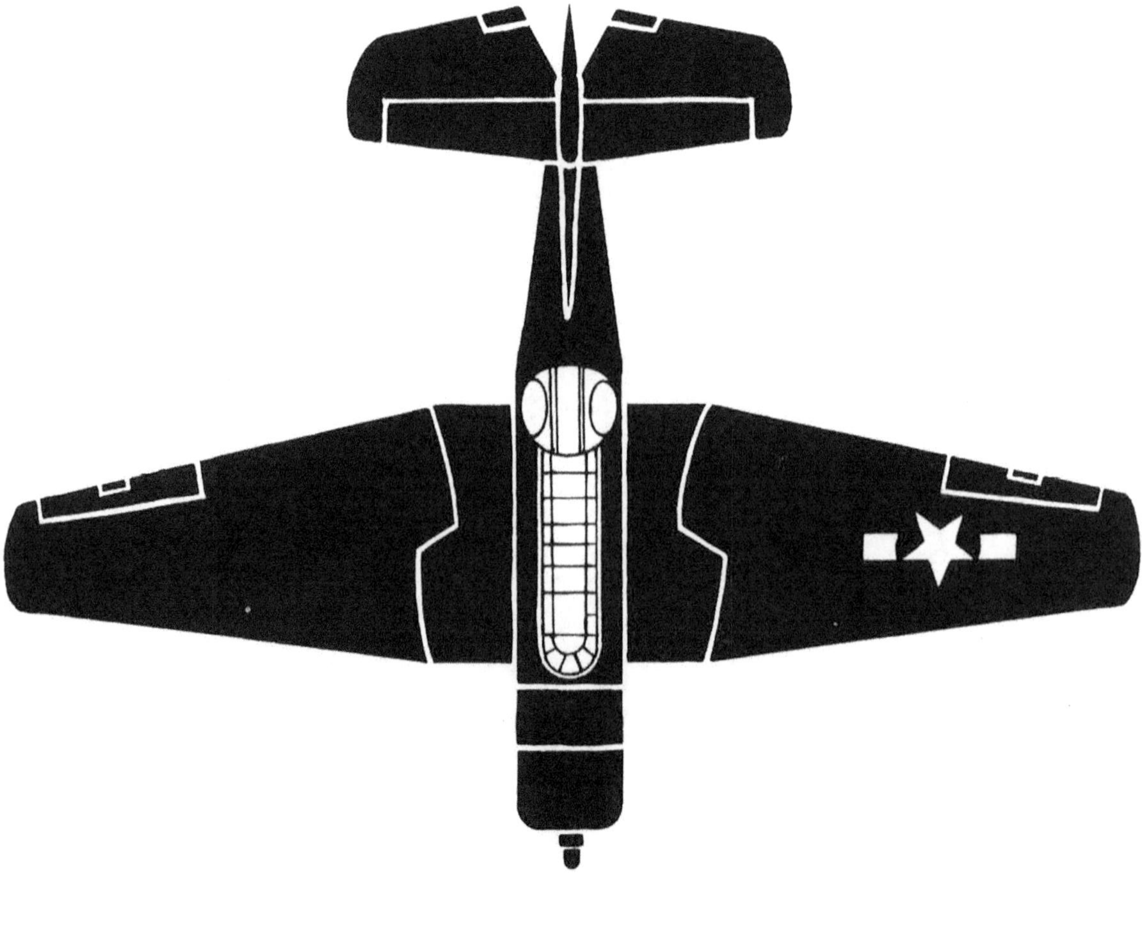

Section I
AN 01-190EB-1
Par. 3, 4

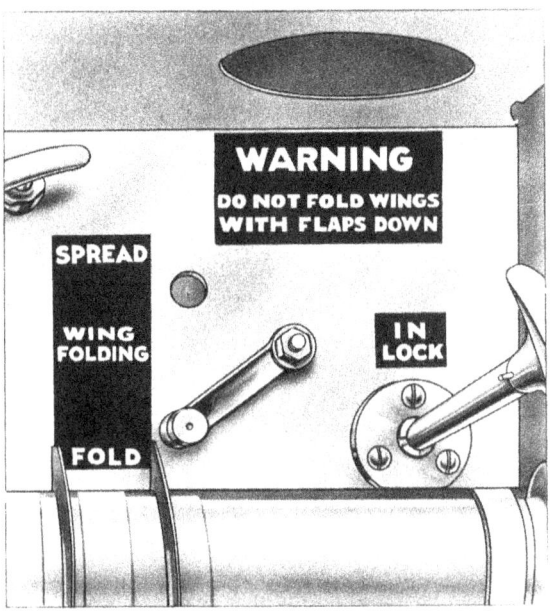

Figure 30 — Wing Folding and Spreading Controls

(4) The position of the wing flaps is indicated by the pointer alongside the wheel indicator.

CAUTION

The wing flaps are not equipped with locks for holding them in the DOWN position, but depend on the hydraulic pressure in the wing flap actuating cylinders remaining constant. If there is a leak in the wing flap hydraulic circuit, the slip-stream may force the flaps UP. If it is felt that all the available pressure will be needed to lower the flaps and keep them down while landing, use the emergency "T" handle to lower the landing gear. No other system is affected by the "T" control and this will avoid using up the reserve supply of pressure in the accumulator, which normally is sufficient to operate the wing flap cylinders and hold the flaps down.

e. WING FOLDING AND SPREADING CONTROLS.

(1) The wing outer panels are spread or folded by hydraulic cylinders and controlled by a selector valve lever on the control panel above the starboard rudder pedal. Two other cylinders move the wing lock pins into locking position when the outer panels are spread. These pins in turn are held in place by safety pins which are actuated mechanically with the "T" handle, mounted just to the right of the selector valve lever. The wing panels should not be folded with the flaps down.

(2) Two warning devices indicate when the wing panels are not locked. The red flags near the leading edge of the wing and adjacent to the folding axis stick up through the wing skin until the outer wing panels are fully extended, the winglock pins in place and locked with the safety locking pins. During the spreading operation, the warning horn (commonly called the Howler) begins to sound as the outer wing panels reach the last 40 degrees of spread, and continues to sound a warning until they are fully spread and locked in position, with the winglock pins home and the safety lock pins in. The Howler warns in the same manner at the beginning of the folding operation.

4. MOVEMENTS OF PERSONNEL.

a. No provision is made for movement of the personnel between the pilot's compartment and other compartments in the airplane, during flight.

b. Movement is unrestricted in the bombardier's compartment and from there it is possible to enter the middle compartment or the turret at any time.

c. ACCESS TO THE TURRET.

(1) Unlatch and pull down the armor plate.

(2) Face aft, rest the back against the armor plate and slide the body up into the turret, holding on the sides of the bullet-proof glass frame.

(3) When seated, raise the feet to the ledge provided for this purpose.

(4) Pull the armor plate up until the latch holds it in the "UP" position.

CAUTION

Be careful when entering the turret not to pull on cables, conduits or other installations which might be damaged.

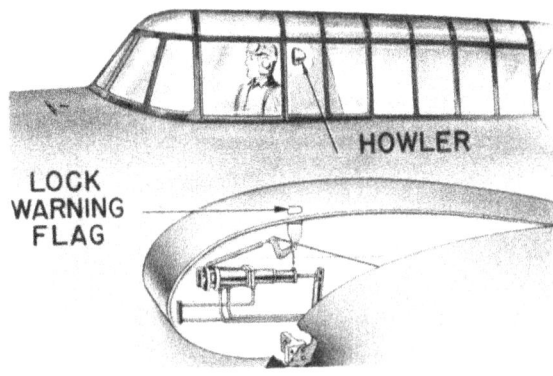

Figure 31 — Wing Fold Warnings

Figure 32 — Movement of Personnel

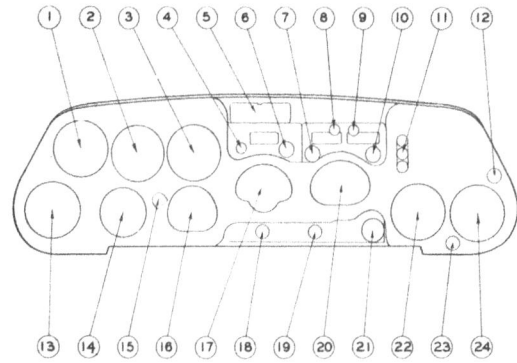

1. Manifold Pressure Gage
2. Altimeter
3. Air Speed Indicator
4. Rudder Sensitivity Trim
5. Airspeed Correction Chart
6. Rudder Trim Control
7. Aileron Trim Control
8. Aileron Sensitivity Control
9. Elevator Sensitivity Control
10. Elevator Trim Control
11. Radio Altimeter Lights
12. AN/APN-1 Altimeter Range Control
13. Tachometer
14. Climb Indicator
15. Chart Board Light
16. Turn and Bank Indicator
17. Directional Gyro
18. Directional Gyro Control
19. Automatic Pilot Control Switch
20. Bank and Climb Gyro
21. Bank and Climb Gyro Control
22. AN/APN-1 Limit Switch
23. AN/APN-1 Altimeter Control Switch
24. AN/APN-1 Altimeter

Figure 33 — Pilot's Instrument Panel — Top Center

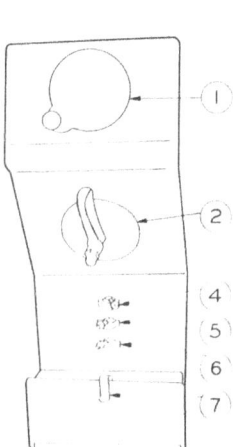

1. Remote Indicating Compass Indicator
2. Fuel Selector Valve
4. Left Droppable Tank Switch
5. Center Droppable Tank Switch
6. Right Droppable Tank Switch
7. Spare Bulb Container

Figure 34 — Pilot's Instrument Panel — Lower Center

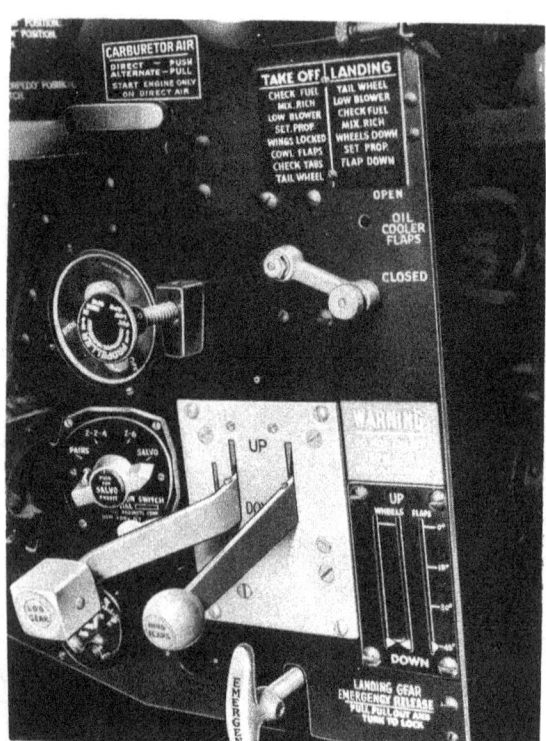

1. Carburetor Air Control
2. Take-off and Landing Check-off List
3. Ignition Switch
4. Oil Cooler Flap Control
5. Propeller Control
6. R. P. Selector Switch
7. Landing Gear Control
8. Wing Flaps Control
9. Thermometer, Outside Air
10. Main Wheels Position Indicator
11. Flaps Position Indicator
12. Emergency Landing Gear Control

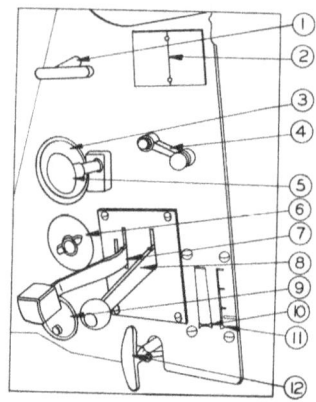

Figure 35 — Pilot's Instrument Panel — Lower Port

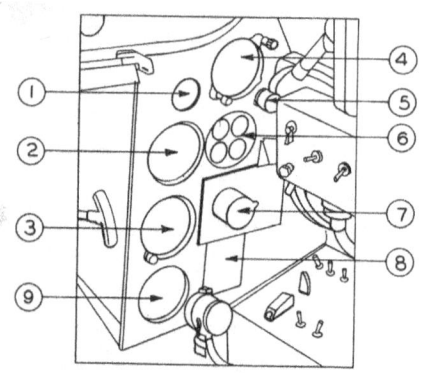

1. Oxygen Flow Indicator
2. Unit Engine Gage
3. Accelerometer
4. Clock
5. Bomb Door Warning Light
6. Fuel Quantity Indicator
7. Wing Gun Charger (Earlier Model Airplanes)
8. Fuel Quantity Gage Compensation Chart
9. Cylinder Engine Gage

Figure 36 — Pilot's Instrument Panel — Lower Starboard

1. Automatic Pilot Gage
2. Stowage Container
3. Autopilot Valve
4. Tail Wheel Caster Lock Control
5. Auxiliary Fuel Pump Switch
6. Arresting Hook Control
7. Rudder Tab Control
8. Engine Control Quadrant
9. Radar, Pilot Viewer Bracket
10. Aileron Tab Control
11. Elevator Tab Control

Figure 37 — Pilot's Cockpit — Port Side

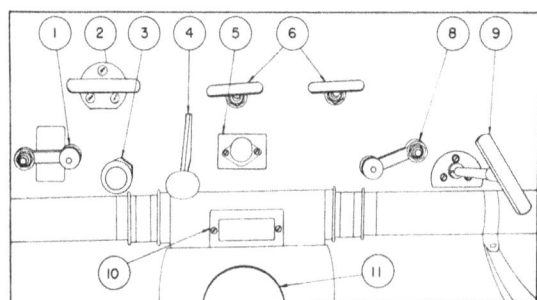

1. Cowl Flap Control
2. Emergency Bomb Release
3. Fuel Strainer Control
4. Bomb Door Control
5. Compass Light
6. Wing Droppable Fuel Tank Control
8. Wing Folding Control
9. Wing Lock Control
10. Indicating Compass Correction Card
11. Remote Indicating Compass Indicator

Figure 38 — Pilot's Sub Panel

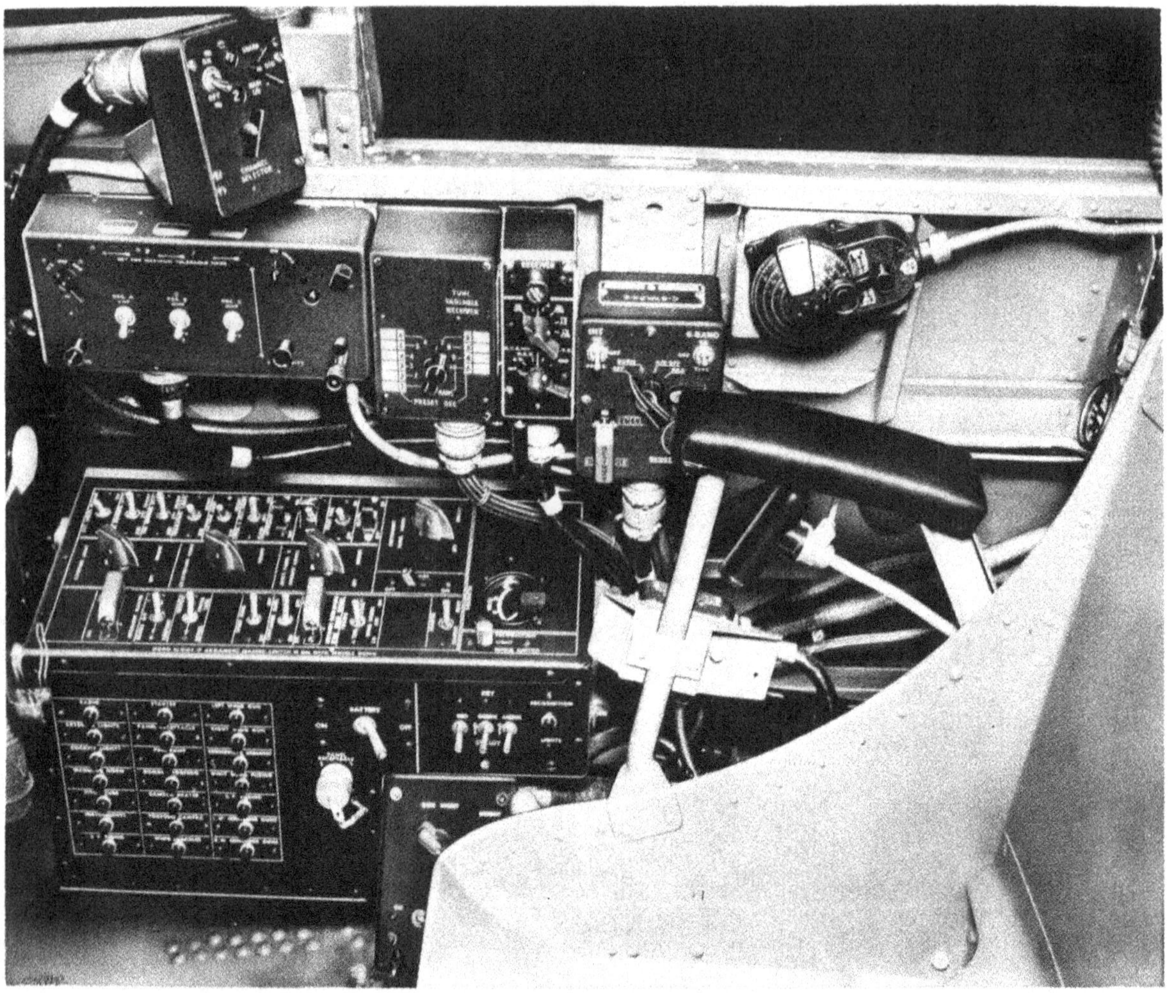

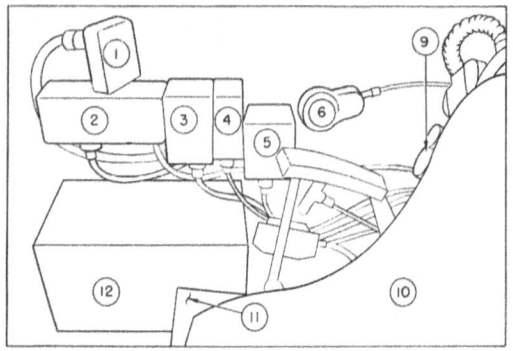

1. ARC-1 Control
2. ARC-5 Control
3. ATC Transmitter Control
4. ARB Receiver Control
5. APX-2 Control
6. ARB Remote Tuner
9. Oxygen Flow Control
10. Pilot's Seat
11. Gun Sight Control Box
12. Electrical Distribution Panel

Figure 39 — Pilot's Cockpit Starboard Side

Section I

AN 01-190EB-1

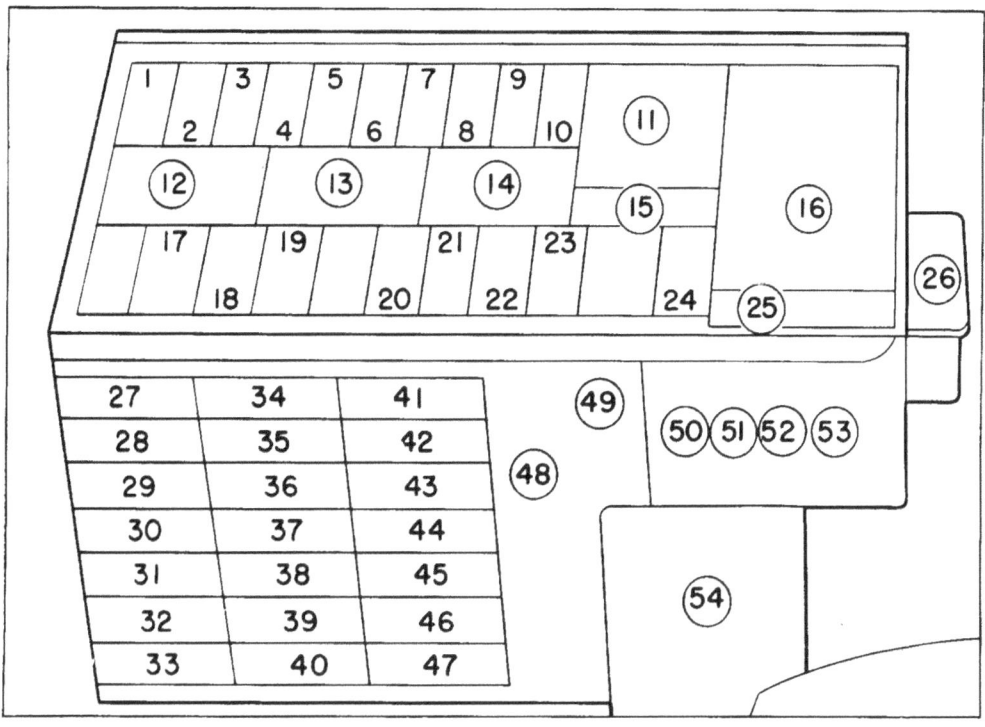

1. External Light Master Switch
2. Wing Running Lights Switch
3. Tail Running Lights Switch
4. Formation Lights Switch
5. Section Lights Switch
6. Formation and Section Lights Switch
7. Approach Light Switch
8. Radio Master Switch
9. Pitot Tube Switch
10. Heater Switch
11. Instrument Panel Lights Rheostat
12. Compass Light Rheostat.
13. Chartboard Light Rheostat
14. Electric Panel and Cockpit Lights Rheostat
15. Primer Switch
16. Voltmeter.
17. Armament Master Switch
18. Bomb-Torpedo-R. P. Switch
19. Bomb-Torpedo-Smoke Tank Switch
20. Wing Guns Switch
21. Container Guns Switch
22. Container Guns-Radar-Wing Bombs Release Switch
23. Wing Bombs Fuzing Switch
24. Starter Switch
25. Recognition Light Switch Keying Switch
26. Oil Dilution Switch
27. Radio Reset Button
28. External Lights
29. Cockpit Lights Reset Button
30. Warning Horn Reset Button
31. Pitot Tube Reset Button
32. Instrument Reset Button
33. R. P. Firing-Reset Button
34. Starter Reset Button
35. Panel Receptacle Reset Button
36. Fuel Pump Reset Button
37. Bomb-Torpedo Reset Button
38. Camera Heater Reset Button
39. Torpedo Camera Reset Button
40. Wing Shackles Reset Button
41. Left Wing Gun Reset Button
42. Right Wing Gun Reset Button
43. Bombardier's Armament Reset Button
44. Wing Bomb Fuzing Reset Button
45. R. P. Fuzing Reset Button
46. Left Wing Container Guns Reset Button
47. Right Wing Container Guns Reset Button
48. Panel Receptacle
49. Battery Switch
50. Recognition Red Light Switch
51. Recognition Green Light Switch
52. Recognition Amber Light Switch
53. Recognition Lights Reset Button
54. Torpedo Director-Gun Sight Rheostat

Figure 40 — Pilot's Electrical Distribution Panel

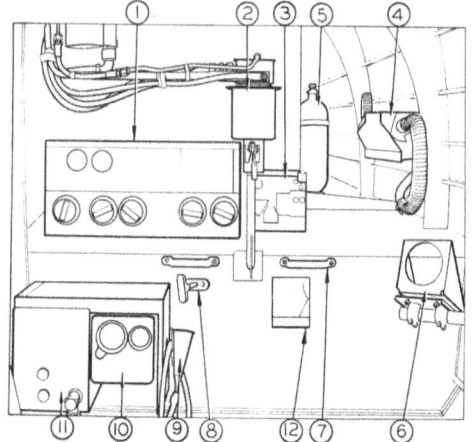

1. ATC Transmitter
2. Turret Slip Ring
3. ARB Receiver
4. Heater (Serial Nos. 23314 to 23656, 68062 to 69538, 85459 to 85780 inclusive)
5. Oxygen Bottle
6. Radar Scope Bracket
7. Catapult Hand Grip
8. Bomb Door Control
9. Relief Tube
10. Instrument Panel
11. Electrical Panel
12. Bomb Bay Window

Figure 41 — Bombardier's Compartment — Front

AN 01-190EB-1

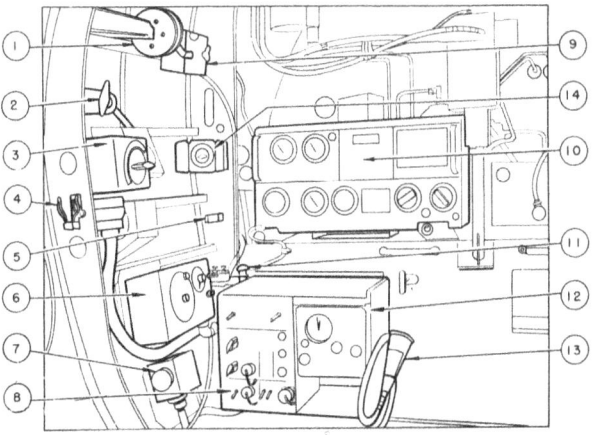

1. Smoke Tank Reel
2. Smoke Tank Control
3. Station Distributor
4. Microphone
5. Firing Key
6. Intervalometer
7. Interphone Control
8. Electrical Panel
9. Turret Power Switch
10. Transmitter
11. Sending Key
12. Instrument Panel (Earlier Airplanes only)
13. Relief Tube
14. Oxygen Flow Indicator

Figure 42 — Bombardier's Compartment — Port Side

SECTION II
NORMAL OPERATING INSTRUCTIONS

1. BEFORE ENTERING PILOT'S COMPARTMENT:

a. FLIGHT LIMITATIONS AND RESTRICTIONS.

(1) Permissible accelerations and speeds at various gross weights are as follows:

Gross Weight Pounds	Permissible Positive Acceleration	Permissible Negative Acceleration	Permissible Speed Knots (Indicated)
13,000 and less	4.6g	2.0g	315
13,500	4.4g	2.0g	315
14,000	4.2g	2.0g	315
14,500	4.0g	2.0g	315
15,000	3.8g	2.0g	305
15,500	3.6g	2.0g	295
16,000	3.4g	2.0g	285
16,500	3.2g	2.0g	275
17,000	3.0g	1.9g	265
17,500	2.8g	1.8g	255
18,000	2.6g	1.7g	245

(2) When turbulent conditions are known to exist, or can be expected, speeds must be reduced and pull-outs must be executed with due regard for increased acceleration resulting from this turbulence.

(3) Do not use flaps at speeds greater than 130 knots (150 mph) indicated air speed.

(4) Do not use full throw of ailerons at speeds greater than 200 knots (230 mph) indicated air speed. At higher speeds aileron deflection shall be limited to that attainable using a control force no greater than that required for full throw at 200 knots (230 mph).

(5) Do not lower landing gear in excess of 200 knots (230 mph) IAS, and do not raise in excess of 150 knots (173 mph) IAS.

(6) All Acrobatics are strictly prohibited in this airplane.

(7) Voluntary spins are not permitted in this airplane.

(8) Glide bombing may be carried out with bomb bay doors open or closed, with landing gear extended or retracted subject to the speed limitations given above but steep prolonged dives are not permitted in this airplane.

(9) Maximum recommended values of gross weights for various types of operation are as follows:

Landing, Average Fields	15,500 lbs.
Landing, Prepared Runways	16,000 lbs.
Take-off, Prepared Runways	17,600 lbs.
Arrested Landing	15,500 lbs.
Catapulting	18,100 lbs.

These limitations may be supplemented or superseded by instructions included in Service publications.

b. WEIGHT AND BALANCE.—Obtain the take-off gross weight and balance of the airplane. Refer to The Handbook of Weight and Balance Data, AN 01-1B-40.

c. ACCESS TO AIRPLANE.

(1) PILOT'S COCKPIT.—Access to the Pilot's Cockpit may be gained from either the Port or Starboard wing. Either side of the canopy can be unlocked by pressing the knurled push button at the lower forward edge. Either side can be moved independently and can be locked closed, open or in three intermediate positions.

(2) MIDDLE COMPARTMENT.—The enclosure of the second cockpit can be opened from the outside by reaching through the small door below the starboard cabin rail and operating the handle on the hatch section of the enclosure.

(3) BOMBARDIER'S COMPARTMENT.—Entrance to the bombardier's compartment is made through the door in the starboard side of the fuselage.

2. ON ENTERING THE COCKPIT.

a. PILOT'S SEAT—The Pilot's Seat is equipped with a vertical adjustment lever attached to the right side of the seat.

The shoulder type harness is adjusted with a lever attached to the left side of the seat.

b. WING.—SPREADING & FOLDING.

The successive steps in the spreading and folding operations are as follows:

SPREADING:

1. Disconnect the wing tie-back cables at the stabilizers.

2. If the hand pump is being used, put the hand pump selector valve lever at the position marked GENERAL.

3. Move the wing flap control lever to UP position.

4. Move the wing folding control lever to SPREAD position.

5. When the wing panels are fully spread and the wing lock pins in locking position, PUSH the wing lock safety pin "T" handle FULL IN and rotate clockwise.

Figure 43 — Access to Cockpit

6. Look to see if the red flags have disappeared into the wing skin.

If the "T" handle cannot be pushed in easily, it indicates that the wing lock pin is not fully IN which may be due to low pressure in the hydraulic system. With the hand pump selector valve lever in the GENERAL position, build up the pressure with the hand pump. If ample pressure is indicated and the "T" handle cannot be pushed all the way in without undue effort, have the alignment of the wing lock fittings checked.

FOLDING:

1. Move wing flap control lever to UP position.

2. Pull out safety locking pins by rotating the "T" handle counterclockwise and pulling it all the way out.

3. Move the control lever on the wing folding selector valve to FOLD position.

4. When the wing panels have folded all the way back, fasten the tie-back cables to the stabilizers.

If the hydraulic system is not in operation the wing panels can be folded manually by releasing the safety pins, using the "T" handle, and disengaging the wing lock pins with the hand lever. An extension handle for manual operation will be found just below the wing locking cylinder.

CAUTION

Do not reverse the wing folding lever before the spreading or folding operation is completed.

Do not try to hurry the spreading or folding by pushing or pulling on the wing panels.

1. Wing Tie-Back Cables
2. Wing Folding Spreading and Locking Controls
3. Landing Gear and Wing Flap Control Unit

Figure 44 — Wing Folding and Spreading

c. STANDARD CHECK FOR ALL FLIGHTS.
  (1) Fuel & Oil.
  (2) Controls & Brake.
  (3) Battery.
  (4) Communications.
  (5) Oxygen.
  (6) Ammunition.
  (7) Instrument Setting.
    (*a*) Altimeter.
    (*b*) Clock.
  (8) Pyrotechnics.

d. SPECIAL CHECK FOR NIGHT FLIGHTS.
  (1) Running Lights.
  (2) Formation Lights.
  (3) Section Light.
  (4) Recognition Lights.
  (5) Approach Light.
  (6) Lights—Pilot's Cockpit.
  (7) Lights—Bombardier's Compartment.
  (8) Aldis Lamp—Bombardier's Compartment.

3. FUEL SYSTEM MANAGEMENT.

a. PROCEDURE TO USE WHEN CHANGING TANKS.

(1) Do not fully exhaust one fuel supply before making the shift to an alternate tank.

(2) If in flight, set mixture control in AUTOMATIC RICH position.

(3) Switch auxiliary fuel pump ON until change is completed. When shifting to a droppable tank, leave switch on for at least one minute after effecting shift to prevent loss of fuel pressure and engine failure.

(4) Turn tank selector valve to the desired tank. If a droppable tank is to be used, switch the toggle switch controlling the valve for that tank to ON. If a droppable tank has just been used, switch the toggle switch controlling the valve for that tank to OFF.

b. ORDER IN WHICH TO USE TANKS.—
  Warm-Up—Center Main Tank.
  Take-Off—Left or Right Main tank. Switch to Center Main Tank as soon as a safe altitude has been reached for the initial stages of flight.
  Sustained Flight—Fuel from Droppable tanks, if carried, should be used first.
  Landing—Left or Right Main Tank.

CAUTION

It is important that fuel be used in the above order to preclude the possibility of engine failure during take-off, due to the accumulation of water in the Center Main Tank in earlier airplanes; or fire, due to the overflow of the vapor elimination system return fuel which returns to the Center Main Tank. When Droppable Tanks are used and Center Main Tank is full, switch to Center Main Tank at frequent intervals to prevent overflow of the vapor vent return fuel.

c. The approximate return fuel flow in vapor elimination system is from one to ten gallons per hour.

4. STARTING ENGINE.

a. Chock wheels and hold brakes.

b. Check fuel supply of all tanks.

c. Set the controls in the following positions:

(1) Ignition switch, accessory switches—OFF.
(2) Mixture—IDLE CUT OFF.
(3) Supercharger—LOW.
(4) Propeller—LOW PITCH (Full IN position).
(5) Cowl flaps—OPEN.
(6) Throttle—CRACKED.
(7) Auxiliary Fuel Pump—ON.

d. Pull the propeller slowly by hand in the normal direction of rotation through at least three complete revolutions.

e. Immediately before starting, adjust the following controls, as noted:

(1) Carburetor air—DIRECT.
(2) Oil cooler flap—CLOSED. If the temperature of the oil is less than -7°C (19°F) the oil should be preheated, unless it was diluted prior to the last stop.
(3) Throttle—set for a maximum of 1200 RPM.
(4) Fuel supply cock—on tank desired.
(5) Battery switch—ON (if no other source of electricity is available).

Figure 45 — Temperature and Pressure Gage

f. Starter switch—STARTER (15 sec.) During the last 3 to 5 seconds, the electric primer should be moved to ON. The amount of priming may be varied as indicated by experience. If the engine is warm, priming may not be necessary.

g. Move starter switch to MESH.

h. After the propeller has turned two revolutions, turn the ignition switch to ON-BOTH.

i. As the engine starts to fire and before the priming charge is used up, move the mixture control to AUTOMATIC RICH position. As the carburetor starts to function, decrease the priming until the engine is running smoothly on the carburetor.

j. Check fuel pressure—16 to 18½ p.s.i.

k. DO NOT PUMP THE THROTTLE.—This practice causes a wide and rapid variation of the fuel-air ratio and may result in serious backfiring during the starting operation.

l. Stop the engine if the oil pressure gage does not register 40 p.s.i. within 30 seconds after starting.

m. If engine cuts out, immediately return mixture control to IDLE CUT-OFF and switch auxiliary fuel pump OFF. Should the engine refuse to start after two attempts, move the mixture control to cut off, shut off the ignition switch, open the throttle wide and pull propeller by hand in the direction of normal rotation to clear the engine of excess fuel. Repeat the starting procedure.

CAUTION

Before starting engine, be sure fire fighting equipment is convenient. The airplane is not equipped with fire extinguishers.

5. ENGINE WARM-UP.

a. Set the controls as follows:

(1) Fuel Selector Valve—Center Main.
(2) Carburetor Air Control—DIRECT.
(3) Cowl Flaps—OPEN.
(4) Oil Cooler flap—CLOSED. Slowly open when oil temperature reaches 75° C (167° F).
(5) Mixture Control—AUTOMATIC RICH.
(6) Propeller Governor—LOW (Full IN position).
(7) Operate at 1200 RPM until the oil temperature gage registers at least 30°C (86°F). If the oil dilution system has been used prior to stopping, the engine speed can be increased at the minimum oil temperature of 30°C (86°F). Reduce engine speed if cylinder head temperature rises above 218° C (424°F).

Slowly increase the engine speed to 1500 RPM. If the oil pressure fluctuates, operate at 1200 RPM until the speed may be increased without oil pressure fluctuation.

CAUTION

Do not operate a cold engine at high RPM.

6. ENGINE GROUND TEST.

a. During taxiing operations, the mixture control should be in the AUTOMATIC RICH position and the propeller governor control should be in high RPM position.

b. Check fuel and oil pressure. After the engine has been given a thorough warm-up, open the throttle to 30" Hg manifold pressure. If the oil pressure drops or fluctuates, reduce speed and continue the warm-up. Fuel pressure should be 16 to 18½ p.s.i. If below this pressure at 1800 RPM, reset within allowable range before flight.

c. Magneto Check. This should be made by taking a flash reading while operating on one magneto at a time. It must be remembered, that atmospheric conditions will influence the readings obtained, but under normal conditions, a drop of 75 to 100 RPM might reasonably be expected. An excessive drop in RPM indicates improper functioning of the magneto assembly, or malfunctioning of the spark plugs. Operate on a single magneto for as short a time as possible and return switch to the BOTH position after each check, to allow the engine to clear out.

d. Check idle mixture adjustment by clearing engine briefly at 1800 RPM. Switch auxiliary fuel pump ON. Then close throttle to idle at 600 RPM. Move mixture control lever momentarily, but with smooth, steady pull into IDLE CUT-OFF. If RPM momentarily increases more than 10, idle mixture is too rich; if RPM drops immediately or remains unchanged, idle mixture may be too lean and should be checked for proper acceleration.

e. Adjust oil cooler flap as oil warms up.

f. CHECK SUPERCHARGER.

(1) BEFORE FLIGHT.—In order to preclude failure of the two-speed supercharger due to accumulation of sludge restricting the movement of the clutches the supercharger clutches shall be shifted to each position, HIGH and LOW for two 30 second periods during warm-up prior to each day's flight.

PROCEDURE:

(*a*) Propeller governor—HIGH RPM (Full IN position).

(*b*) Throttle—1000 RPM.

(*c*) Supercharger Control—Shift rapidly from LOW to HIGH and lock; retain in this position for 30 seconds.

(*d*) Supercharger Control—shift rapidly from HIGH to LOW.

(2) THIRTY HOUR GROUND CHECK OR CLUTCH OPERATION CHECK.—At the completion of 30 hours or whenever it is desired to check the operation of the supercharger clutch the following test shall be made after engine warm-up.

PROCEDURE:

(a) After the engine oil has reached the minimum temperature required for take-off, open the throttle to obtain 1700 rpm and shift from low to high blower.

(b) Adjust the throttle to obtain any manifold pressure between 25 and 30 inches; allow the engine operation to stabilize; then note the rpm at the manifold pressure selected.

(c) Shift to low blower as instructed in paragraph 12.b.(1)(e) of this Section; readjust the throttle to obtain the same manifold pressure selected in high blower; then note the rpm when the engine operation has stabilized. If the rpm for low blower operation is appreciably higher (anywhere from 50 to 150 rpm, depending on atmospheric conditions) than that in high blower, the supercharger is operating satisfactorily.

WARNING

Make certain that the supercharger control is in the "LOW" position when the check is complete.

g. Check Fuel Selector Valve.—Run engine for a full minute on each tank. After check, return the selector valve to the CENTER MAIN TANK.

h. GENERATOR SYSTEM CHECK.

(1) Disconnect external power source if used, and turn on battery switch. With engine idling, turn on a light electrical load such as lights, instruments, etc.

(2) Slowly increase the engine speed and watch the voltmeter for the jump from 24.0 volts to 26.5 volts which should occur below 1400 rpm to indicate the closing of the generator reverse current cutout. (In planes equipped with a volt-ammeter, this will be shown by the indication of current flow on the ammeter. Push the volt-ammeter button to see that the voltage reading is 26.5 at this time.)

(3) As the engine speed is further increased, the voltage should increase from 26.5 to about 28.0 and then remain at 28.0 volts regardless of any further increase in engine in engine speed. (This check can be made with a volt-ammeter by holding the volt-ammeter button in while increasing engine speed.)

NOTE

During flight, a quick check to determine whether or not the generator is supplying power to the electrical system can be made by momentarily turning the battery switch "OFF". Loss of electrical equipment power (instruments, lights, etc.) will mean that the battery alone is supplying electrical power. In that case, every effort should be made to conserve the battery.

i. Check the throttle operation. See that the friction crab is all right and does not slip back from any set position. If it does slip, tighten the adjusting knob on the side of the quadrant.

j. Check the Propeller Governor.—Operate the propeller governor control to make sure that it is functioning properly.

7. TAXIING INSTRUCTIONS.

a. Tail wheel unlocked—cockpit cover locked open.

b. The minimum engine speed when taxiing should be 1000 RPM.

c. Check operation of brakes. A sluggish, "mushy" feeling, with little reactionary force, signifies that the brakes are not in perfect condition.

d. Do not taxi with wings folded, unless absolutely necessary.

CAUTION

Do not taxi with flaps DOWN. Avoid possible damage.

Ground looping characteristics are normal.

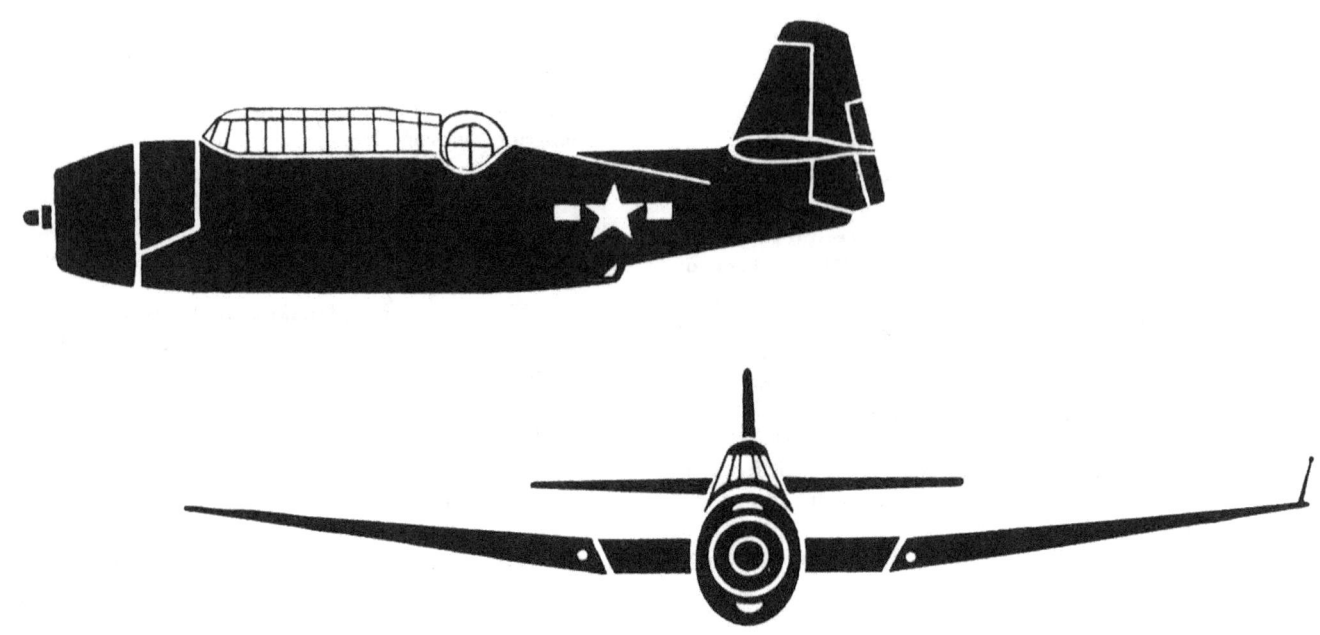

THIS PAGE INTENTIONALLY LEFT BLANK.

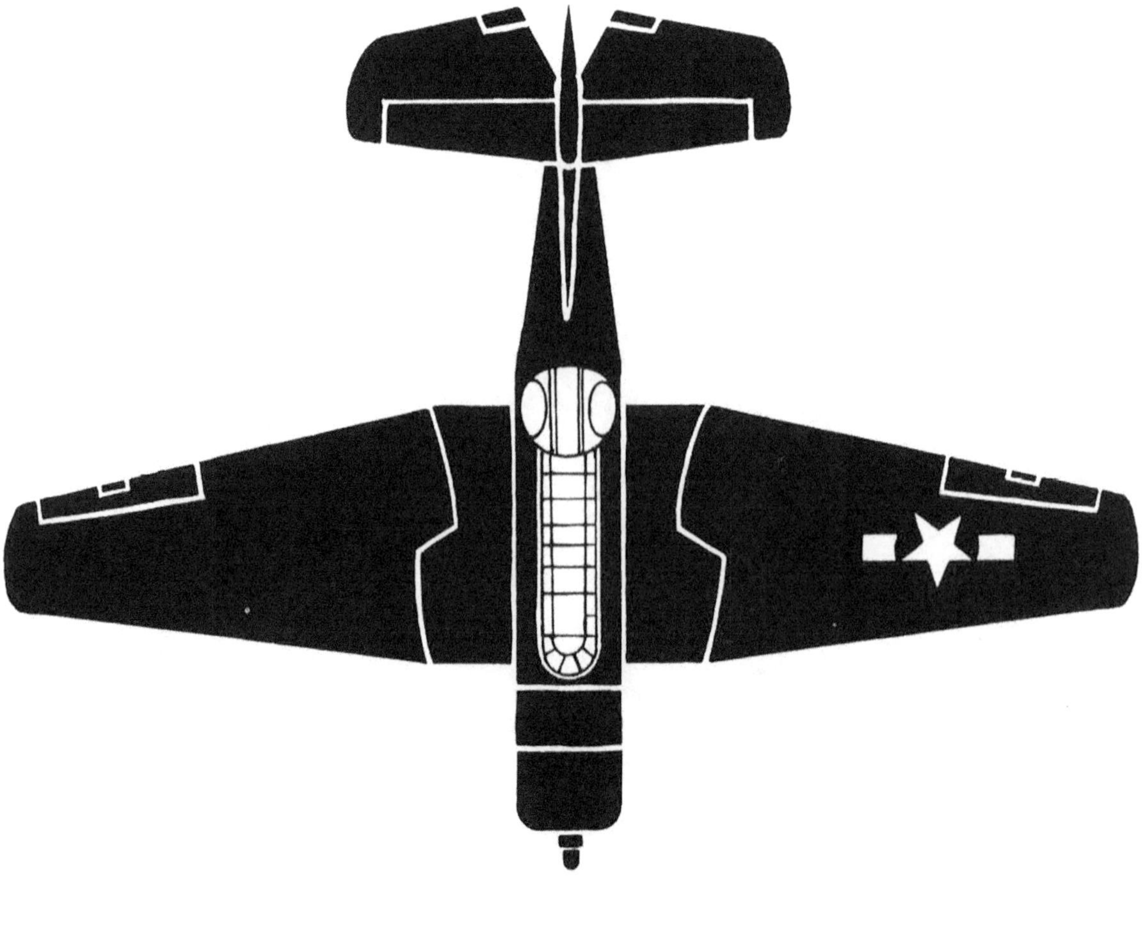

8. EMERGENCY TAKE-OFF.

a. Start engine in the normal manner, then if the engine oil was properly diluted when the engine was previously stopped, the oil pressure should quickly steady itself within the limits set forth in the Power Plant Chart in Section III. If the oil pressure is too high, fluctuates or falls back when the engine RPM is increased, the oil dilution toggle switch may be moved to the ON position for intervals of a few seconds over a period of about fifteen seconds. The oil pressure gage should be watched carefully, as over dilution and low oil pressure is likely to result under these conditions.

b. The airplane may be flown as soon as the oil temperature is 20°C (68°F), the oil pressure is steady, the engine is running smoothly and will "take" the throttle.

c. If the engine oil was NOT diluted prior to the previous stopping, the dilution system MUST NOT BE USED. It will not aid in starting and may cause trouble.

9. TAKE-OFF.

a. Normal Take-Off Check-off List:
  (1) Wings—Spread and locked.
  (2) Bomb Doors—Closed.
  (3) Mixture Control—Auto Rich.
  (4) Blower Control—Low ratio.
  (5) Propeller Control—High RPM.
     (Full IN position).
  (6) Carburetor Air Control—Direct.
  (7) Cowl Flaps—Open.
  (8) Oil Cooler Flaps—Open.
  (9) Fuel Tank Selector—Left or Right Main Tanks.
  (10) Elevator Tab—Neutral.
  (11) Rudder Tab—1° Nose right.
  (12) Aileron Tab—Neutral.
  (13) Tail Wheel Caster—Locked.
  (14) Cabin Hood—Locked open.
  (15) Manifold Pressure—Open throttle SLOWLY to desired pressure.
  (16) Auxiliary Fuel Pump—ON. Leave ON until normal flight altitude is attained.
  (17) Wing Flaps—Partially lowered (as desired).
  (18) Shoulder harness adjusted and secured.

b. MINIMUM TAKE OFF.—The following will aid if minimum take-off runs are desired:
  (1) Flaps fully lowered.
  (2) Take-off power reached with airplane held by brakes before starting run.

CAUTION

If airplane is not loaded and at a stand still, throttle of 49" Hg may be excessive and cause the airplane to nose over.

  (3) Tail raised by moderate force on controls during first part of run.
  (4) When take-off speed is reached, tail pulled down to reach maximum angle of attack at moment of leaving the ground.
  (5) Wheels raised when clear of ground. Apply brakes to prevent tire wear as the wheels retract into the wheel wells.
  (6) After reaching an airspeed of about 100 knots (115mph), flaps raised and airplane retrimmed, longitudinally at the same time.

WARNING

There is a considerable loss in lift when the flaps are raised, as well as a nose heavy shift in trim. It is recommended that pilots investigate this characteristic at an altitude above 500 ft. during the initial familiarization period.

c. Catapult Take-Off.
  (1) Adjust seat, headrest and safety belt.
  (2) Flaps full down.
  (3) Elevator tab about $1\frac{1}{2}$° NOSE DOWN.
  (4) Rudder tab about 3° NOSE RIGHT.
  (5) Aileron tab about 1° LEFT WING DOWN.
  (6) Stick in neutral position.
  (7) Throttle friction adjustment snug.
  (8) Use full manifold pressure.

d. Refer to Power Plant Chart, Flight Operating Instruction Chart, Take-Off Climb and Landing Chart.

10. ENGINE FAILURE DURING TAKE-OFF.

If the engine fails immediately after take-off, proceed as follows:

a. Immediately depress the nose, in order to maintain flying speed.

b. If possible to land within airport boundary, land straight ahead.

c. If it is too late to land within the airport boundary, retract the landing gear and land off the field, straight ahead. *Do not attempt to turn back into the field.*

d. If there is time
  (1) Lower flaps.
  (2) Turn off fuel.
  (3) Switch off ignition.
  (4) Drop wing tanks, if carried.

11. CLIMB.

a. With an increase of altitude, the throttle must be gradually opened until, at the critical altitude of the engine without further supercharging, it is fully open.

b. For climbs at Normal Rated Power shift from LOW to HIGH blower at 10,000 ft. For climbs at Military Power shift from LOW to HIGH blower at 10,500 ft.

c. Use AUTOMATIC LEAN mixture for climbing at all powers provided that cylinder head temperature can be maintained below limits with the cowl flaps no more than half open. If temperatures are close to limits, increase air speed slightly to improve cooling. As a last measure shift mixture to AUTOMATIC RICH if temperatures cannot be maintained below limits. Adjust the oil cooler flaps as necessary to maintain specified limits.

d. Consult the Power Plant Chart for power settings and temperature limits.

e. Best Climbing Speed.—Indicated air speeds for the best rate of climb will vary with the load carried by the airplane. For the best climbing airspeed under various gross weights, refer to Take-Off, Climb and Landing Chart.

12. GENERAL FLYING CHARACTERISTICS.

a. AIRPLANE.

(1) Longitudinal stability is normal with the center of gravity as far aft as 29.5% M.A.C. Elevator forces are comparatively heavy. When the cowl flaps are opened the airplane becomes slightly tail heavy. The raising of the alighting gear causes tail heaviness and the lowering of the alighting gear causes nose heaviness. Do not lower alighting gear at I.A.S. exceeding 200 knots (235 mph.). As the flaps are lowered there is a tail heavy shift in trim. Do not lower flaps at speeds greater than 130 knots (150 mph.).

WARNING

It is important that the pilot should familiarize himself with the foregoing characteristics prior to night and low visibility landings and take-offs.

(2) Lateral stability is normal in the clean condition and neutral in the landing condition. Aileron control is comparatively heavy at small angles of deflection and somewhat less so at large angles. Restrict full throw of the ailerons to speeds under 200 knots (235 mph.). At higher speeds, aileron deflection shall be limited to that attainable using a control force no greater than that required for full throw at 200 knots (235 mph.).

(3) Directional stability is normal in the clean condition and weak in the landing condition, decreasing to zero at full yaw, where under some conditions the rudder will reverse. At large angles of yaw a tail heavy shift in trim occurs.

WARNING

Since control is greatly reduced in side slips at low altitudes in the landing conditions, side slips should not be carried beyond the point where there is a noticeable decrease in rudder force.

b. ENGINE.

(1) USE OF SUPERCHARGER.

(*a*) The engine should be operating in the blower ratios specified in the Power Plant Chart. HIGH blower ratio may be used as indicated in the Power Plant Chart to obtain maximum speeds and rates of climb. It should not be used for cruising at altitudes at which cruising power is available in LOW blower ratio, since fuel economy is inferior to that obtainable in low blower ratio, and the tendency to detonate is greater. It is essential that pilots realize the limitations of the supercharger high speed ratio. For each set of power conditions there is a critical altitude for the supercharger low ratio, above which, at the RPM specified, the manifold pressure and power will drop off gradually with increased altitude, even at full throttle. The use of the supercharger high ratio for the same power conditions below the altitude specified would result in considerable loss of power. This loss is attributable both to the additional power required to drive the supercharger high ratio and to the increased mixture temperature (not apparent on the indicator as normally located) that results from the use of the supercharger high ratio.

(*b*) THE SUPERCHARGER HIGH RATIO SHOULD NEVER BE USED FOR TAKE-OFF. While in supercharger low ratio, the engine should be operated as a single-speed supercharged engine.

(*c*) During flight, if tactically feasible, operating time in high blower should be followed by twice as much time in low blower. In the event of prolonged flight in supercharger high ratio, it is recommended that the supercharger be shifted to low ratio every two hours for approximately 15 minutes. This is necessary to insure best operation of the two-speed supercharger. Do not shift the supercharger control in flight more often than five minute intervals, except in an emergency, but at least once every five hours. Operation in supercharger low ratio may be continued as long as desired.

Note

Do not shift supercharger with engine speed above 1800 RPM.

(*d*) To change from LOW to HIGH ratio the following procedure shall be used in the sequence given:

1. Mixture Control—AUTO RICH.

2. Auxiliary Pump—ON.

3. Reduce throttle setting as necessary to prevent exceeding desired manifold pressure in the higher ratio.

4. Reduce RPM to 1700 with propeller governor.

5. Supercharger Control—Move rapidly from LOW to HIGH position and lock.

6. Readjust the RPM, throttle setting, mixture control and auxiliary fuel pump as necessary to obtain the desired power.

(*e*) To change from HIGH to LOW ratio the following procedure shall be used in the sequence given:

1. Reduce RPM to 1500 RPM or less.

2. Supercharger Control—move rapidly from HIGH to LOW position and lock.

3. Readjust RPM, throttle, and mixture control as necessary to obtain desired power.

(*f*) If a shift to HIGH ratio is attempted and the clutch does not engage or if for some reason the HIGH ratio clutch becomes disengaged, close the throttle to 800-1000 RPM or as low as possible, shift to LOW, speed engine up to at least 1700 RPM and shift to HIGH using the procedure described above.

(*g*) Changes from one supercharger ratio to another should be made quickly, without pausing between high and low positions. The supercharger control lever must be securely locked at the extremity of its travel in either the high or low position to insure complete and positive clutch engagement. High supercharger clutch shifts should not be attempted at engine speeds below 1700 RPM, and while shifting is permissible at speeds above 1700 RPM, it is recommended that all shifts be effected at 1700 RPM whenever possible. During flight, do not shift into the same ratio more than once within a five minute interval. This need not be observed during ground operation at low engine speeds, i.e., low clutch loads.

(2) CHANGING POWER CONDITIONS.—In order to prevent excessive pressures within the cylinders, the following procedures shall always be used when changing power:

INCREASING ENGINE POWER.

(*a*) Adjust the mixture control for the power condition desired, as specified in the Power Plant Chart.

(*b*) Adjust propeller control to obtain the desired RPM.

(*c*) Adjust throttle to obtain the desired manifold pressure.

DECREASING ENGINE POWER.

(*a*) Adjust throttle to obtain the desired manifold pressure.

(*b*) Adjust propeller control to obtain the desired RPM.

(*c*) Adjust mixture control for the power conditions desired, as specified in the Power Plant Chart.

(*d*) Close throttle momentarily to insure release of mixture control over-ride valve.

(*e*) Readjust throttle to desired manifold pressure.

(3) CRUISING.

(*a*) While cruising may be conducted at any engine power and RPM, below rated power and RPM, if fuel economy is of importance and if it is tactically feasible to do so, cruising operations should be conducted in a range not to exceed 65 per cent of normal rated power.

(*b*) The engine should be operated in Automatic Lean except when conditions are such that a cylinder head temperature of 232°C (450°F) is exceeded. In such cases, Automatic Rich should be used.

(*c*) Manual leaning beyond Automatic Lean to the point of engine roughness, is permissible at 50% power and below for minimum fuel consumption.

(*d*) The cruising manifold pressure-RPM relationships, specified in the Power Plant Chart, should not be exceeded.

(*e*) Propeller pitch limitations for this installation preclude the use of the low cruising RPM conditions on the Power Plant Chart, at altitudes appreciably above sea level.

13. MANEUVERS PROHIBITED.

a. Aileron roll.

b. Snap roll.

c. Immelmann turn.

d. Inverted flight.

e. Intentional spins.

14. STALLS.

a. The stall warning is less pronounced than in the average airplane. Due to the variable loading conditions, the pilot should become thoroughly familiar with the peculiarities of the stall and the recovery characteristics as soon as possible.

b. Recovery is greatly expedited by rapid and full control movements.

WARNING

Do not stall the airplane at low altitudes, since considerable altitude may be lost before complete recovery can be effected.

15. SPINS.

a. Voluntary spins in this airplane are not permitted.

b. Recovery from an inadvertently entered spin may be accomplished by the standard spin recovery technique, described in the Current Bureau of Aeronautics Technical Order on the subject, since the airplane does not have any peculiarities requiring any deviation from this technique.

c. All control movements should be smooth, but rapid.

16. ACROBATICS.

All acrobatics are strictly prohibited in this airplane.

17. DIVING.

a. Steep prolonged dives are not permissible with this airplane.

b. The Avenger is an excellent torpedo glide bomber, but like all airplanes, it has certain definite restrictions which must not be exceeded. Glide bombing may be carried out with any combination of useful load and with bomb bay doors open or closed, with landing gear extended or retracted provided the following limits are not exceeded:

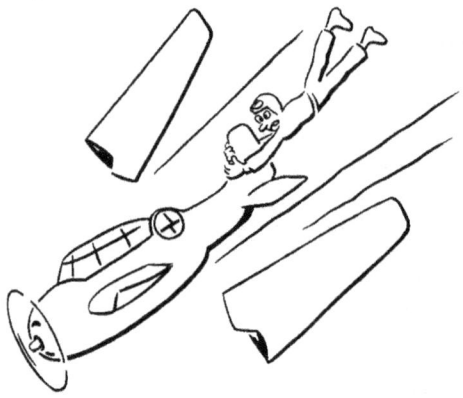

Gross Weight Pounds	Permissible Positive Acceleration	Permissible Negative Acceleration	Permissible Speed Knots (Indicated)
13,000 and less	4.6g	2.0g	315
13,500	4.4g	2.0g	315
14,000	4.2g	2.0g	315
14,500	4.0g	2.0g	315
15,000	3.8g	2.0g	305
15,500	3.6g	2.0g	295
16,000	3.4g	2.0g	285
16,500	3.2g	2.0g	275
17,000	3.0g	1.9g	265
17,500	2.8g	1.8g	255
18,000	2.6g	1.7g	245

WARNING

This airplane will safely withstand existing limiting speeds and accelerations. The only unknown quantity that may have catastrophic results in flight is the magnitude of vertical gusts in turbulent air. When turbulent conditions are known to exist or can be expected, speeds must be reduced and pull-outs must be executed with due regard for increased accelerations resulting from this turbulence. The use of aileron at high speeds or during pull-outs must be undertaken with caution.

c. Fifteen inches of manifold pressure is recommended during prolonged glides to keep the engine warm.

d. Caution should be observed in gliding from a high altitude as manifold pressure will build up rapidly at a constant throttle setting. Caution should also be observed to open throttle very slowly at completion of dive so partly cooled engine will not cut out.

18. APPROACH AND LANDING.

a. CHECK-OFF LIST.
  (1) Bomb doors—CLOSED.
  (2) Alighting gear—DOWN.
  (3) Wing flaps—DOWN.
  (4) Tail wheel caster.
    Shore Base—LOCKED.
    Carrier Base—UNLOCKED after landing gear has been lowered.
  (5) Cabin hood—LOCKED OPEN.

b. SET POWER PLANT CONTROLS AS FOLLOWS:
  (1) Mixture control—AUTOMATIC RICH.
  (2) Carburetor air control—DIRECT.
  (3) Propeller governor control—2400 RPM.
  (4) Fuel tank selector—LEFT or RIGHT MAIN TANK.
  (5) Throttle—AS REQUIRED.
  (6) Blower—LOW RATIO.
  (7) Oil cooler flap—OPEN.

(8) Cowl flaps—In DESIRED POSITION to maintain proper cylinder head temperature.

(9) In the final approach, change the propeller governor control from 2400 RPM to "take-off" RPM (Full IN position).

(10) Auxiliary fuel pump—ON.

(11) If landing cannot be made, open the throttle to obtain take-off power and proceed in accordance with the instructions for take-off, as outlined in this book.

c. CARRIER OPERATION.—Investigation of carrier approaches and arrested landings on the landing platform at the Naval Aircraft Factory has indicated favorable characteristics for these functions. The following comments are added:

Variations in power speed during the approach have less adverse effect than in other types.

A slow condition may be corrected by a large application of throttle without undue probability of excessive over-correction.

Response to application of increased power during the approach is normal. The power loading at gross weights up to and including 15,400 pounds, the maximum investigated, is not excessive.

Waveoffs are satisfactory. Application of full power may be made in response to a waveoff, but the throttle should not be opened so abruptly as to cause faulty engine acceleration.

Visibility during the approach is excellent, especially if the cowl flaps are not fully opened.

For carrier approaches, the tabs should balance the airplane at the approach speed. If so balanced, control forces in a waveoff will not be unreasonable.

While five seconds are required to completely retract the arresting hook, the hook is raised clear of the wires in about 1½ seconds from the time of operating the switch in earlier airplanes.

Arresting hook on later airplanes is not retractable by the pilot.

The airplane may be taxiied with the wings folded before they are secured if necessary.

19. STOPPING ENGINE.

a. After landing, unlock the tail wheel and raise the wing flaps for taxiing.

b. Auxiliary fuel pump—OFF.

c. Set the controls as follows:
 (1) Cowl flaps—OPEN.
 (2) Oil cooler flap—OPEN.
 (3) Propeller control—LOW PITCH.

d. Idle the engine at 800-1000 RPM until the cylinder head temperature drops below 149°C (300°F)

e. Desludging Supercharger (Shore base only)—Desludge the supercharger clutches by operating the engine in each blower position at about 1000 RPM for 30 seconds or more after each flight. The procedure of taxiing back to the line in HIGH blower satisfies this requirement.

f. Increase the engine speed to 1200 RPM and hold for not more than 30 seconds to permit efficient scavenging of the crankcase oil.

g. When a cold weather start is anticipated, the oil dilution system should be used. Refer to "Use of the Oil Dilution System" in this section.

h. Move the mixture control to the idle cut-off position. The engine will stop in a few seconds. The mixture control should be in the idle cut-off position at all times when the engine is not running.

i. After the propeller stops turn the ignition switch to the OFF position. Set throttle control OPEN.

j. Turn all transmitter switches and turret power switches and all other accessory switches OFF.

k. Turn battery switch OFF.

l. Turn fuel selector valve to OFF.

m. Secure plane before leaving it unattended.

20. USE OF OIL DILUTION SYSTEM.

a. GENERAL.—Some TBM-3 airplanes are equipped with an oil dilution system. The oil dilution system should be used just before stopping the engine when a cold weather start is anticipated. It may be used to assist the start when properly used prior to stopping, but should never be used when starting if it was not used prior to stopping. Dilution under the latter conditions will not aid the start and may cause trouble. The oil dilution procedure is as follows:

b. PROCEDURE:

(1) Make sure that the manually operated shut-off valve, at the base of the oil tank, is open.

(2) Set the engine to run at 1000 rpm.

(3) Open the dilution valve by moving the electric toggle switch to the ON position. When the dilution valve is opened, there will be a sharp drop in indicated fuel pressure. Fuel pressure should return to normal immediately upon closing the valve. If it does not, stop the engine immediately and check the valve for leakage.

(4) Hold the dilution valve open for approximately two minutes. Stop engine by moving mixture control to the idle cut off position, then shut off the ignition. Hold dilution valve open until the engine stops turning.

(5) When a cold engine is subsequently started and, after running a short while, the oil pressure starts to fluctuate or drop, the dilution valve shall be opened intermittently for intervals of a few seconds over a period of about fifteen seconds. If the oil pressure still does not become steady, stop the engine and let it rest for approximately five minutes before attempting another start.

(6) When it is assured that the oil pressure is steady, be sure that the dilution switch is in the OFF position and the guard is over the switch.

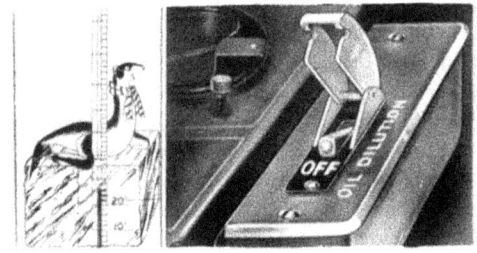

Figure 46 — Oil Dilution Switch

c. PRECAUTIONS:

(1) Do not overdilute.
(2) Guard against fire.
(3) Dilute only when justified by forecast of low temperature, i. e., below —5°C. (23°F).
(4) Allow adequate warm-up before taking off, except in cases of extreme emergency.
(5) Keep oil system free of sludge and water.
(6) Check position of dilution line shut-off cocks.
(7) Since the oil in the propeller is not diluted, care must be taken to determine that the propeller pitch-changing mechanism is operating prior to take-off.

21. USE OF THE CARBURETOR INDUCTION SYSTEM.

The DIRECT position of the air control should be used under all operating conditions if practicable. The ALTERNATE position should be used if the air is very cold or dusty and if icing conditions, heavy rain or other induction hazards are encountered.

The use of the DIRECT position is especially important on take off. If icing conditions exist, the ALTERNATE position may be used just before take-off to clear the induction system, but the DIRECT position should be used for the take-off run. If the necessity should arise for using the ALTERNATE position for take-off, ample allowance should be made for reduced power which will increase the length of the run and decrease the rate of climb.

The DIRECT position increases the power available at any altitude and increases the altitude at which a particular power is available. The power lost by use of the ALTERNATE position may be compensated for by a slight advance of the throttle position. However, when full throttle is approached the compensation cannot be made. Except when full throttle is approached there is no disadvantage in using the ALTERNATE position and there is some evidence that distribution may be improved by shifting to the ALTERNATE position when operating in very cold air.

22. NIGHT FLYING.

a. The battery switch must be ON to operate any lights except the Recognition Lights.

b. The Recognition Lights circuit is connected direct to battery.

c. All other exterior lights are connected in a circuit controlled by the Exterior Lights Master Switch. Both the Master Switch and the Battery Switch must be ON to operate them.

d. The chartboard, the compass and the electrical panel lights in the pilot's cockpit, and the electric panel and the compartment lights in the bombardier's compartment are controlled by rheostats.

e. Recognition lights may be used singly or in combination and may be switched to STEADY, OFF, or KEY. When switches are set to KEY the keying switch is used to flash the lights.

f. The formation and section lights may be flashed by pressing the switch to FLASH and releasing.

g. A white compartment light with a switch mounted on the forward side of the support bracket is located at the top of the bombardier's compartment.

h. Circuit breakers are used instead of the customary fuses. Press button to reset.

i. For carrier operations the approach light switch is OFF and is covered with a guard. It is switched ON automatically when the arresting hook is lowered, and OFF when the hook is retracted. On shore based planes the guard is removed and the approach light is operated manually.

23. BEFORE LEAVING AIRPLANE.

a. PILOT'S COMPARTMENT.

(1) Have wheels chocked if possible.
(2) Fuel Valves OFF.
(3) All light switches and heater switches OFF.
(4) All radio switches OFF.
(5) Battery switch OFF.
(6) Cage Automatic pilot gyros.
(7) If windy, lock flight controls to prevent damage to the control surfaces.
(8) If dusty air conditions prevail set the carburetor air controls to ALTERNATE position.
(9) If oxygen has been used during flight, turn regulator OFF. Demand type regulators should be left with emergency knob OFF, demand knob at NORMAL OXYGEN, and cylinder valve CLOSED.

b. BOMBARDIER'S COMPARTMENT.

(1) All light switches OFF.
(2) All radio switches OFF.
(3) Turn oxygen OFF.

c. TURRET GUNNER.

(1) All light switches OFF.
(2) All power switches OFF.
(3) All radio switches OFF.
(4) Turn oxygen OFF.

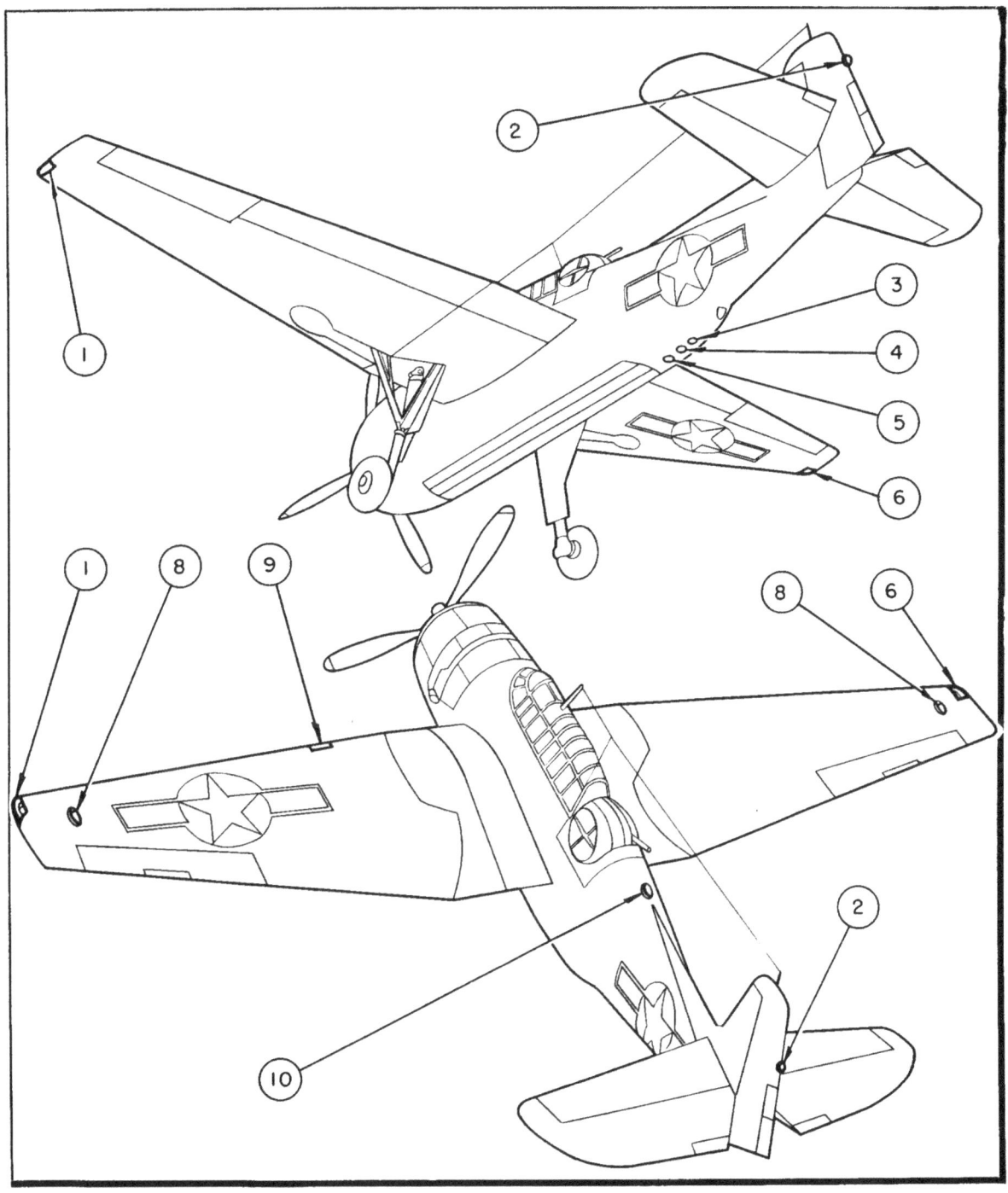

1. Wing Running Light (red)
2. Tail Running Light (white)
3. Recognition Light (amber)
4. Recognition Light (green)
5. Recognition Light (red)
6. Wing Running Light (green)
8. Formation Light (blue)
9. Approach Light (green, amber, red)
10. Section Light (blue)

Figure 47 — External Lights

SECTION III
FLIGHT OPERATING DATA

1. POWER PLANT CHART

a. The Power Plant Chart summarizes the operating limits of the engine. It gives the supercharger setting, manifold pressure, rpm, and altitude range for several different operating conditions. Other conditions affecting the operation of the power plant, such as oil pressures and temperatures are also specified. The rpm and manifold pressures at a given supercharger control setting for take-off and military operation must never be exceeded; the time limit for each of these conditions should not be exceeded. The altitudes corresponding to the supercharger control settings show the approximate altitude for operation at that setting. Operation below the altitude shown for a given supercharger control setting should not be undertaken as less power will be obtained, carburetor air temperatures will be dangerously high, and fuel economy will suffer. When changing power conditions, the controls should be adjusted to the settings appropriate to the new condition in the sequence which follows, in order to avoid excessive pressures within the cylinders:

(1) Increasing power—Mixture, rpm, manifold pressure.

(2) Decreasing power—Manifold pressure, rpm, mixture.

b. In order to obtain the maximum in performance and reliability from the engine, it is recommended that the pilot operate it at its power limits no more often than is necessary for proper familiarity and training.

Section III

AN 01-190EB-1

POWER PLANT CHART

AIRCRAFT MODEL(S)	PROPELLER(S)	ENGINE MODEL(S)
TBM-3	23E50	R2600-20

GAUGE READING	FUEL PRESS.	OIL PRESS.	OIL TEMP.	COOLANT TEMP.		OIL CONS.		
DESIRED	17	85-90	70				MAXIMUM PERMISSABLE DIVING RPM: 3100	
MAXIMUM	18	95	85				MINIMUM RECOMMENDED CRUISE RPM: 1600	
MINIMUM	16	80					MAXIMUM RECOMMENDED TURBO RPM:	
IDLING	11	15					OIL GRADE: 1120, AN-VV-O-446	
							FUEL GRADE: 100/130, SPEC. AN-F-28	

WAR EMERGENCY (COMBAT EMERGENCY)			MILITARY POWER (NON-COMBAT EMERGENCY)			OPERATING CONDITION			NORMAL RATED (MAXIMUM CONTINUOUS)			MAXIMUM CRUISE (NORMAL OPERATION)		
MINUTES			30 MINUTES			TIME LIMIT			UNLIMITED			UNLIMITED		
NOT			248°C			MAX. CYL. HD. TEMP.			232°C	*		218°C		
APPLICABLE			AUTO LEAN			MIXTURE			AUTO LEAN			AUTO LEAN		
			2600			R.P.M.			2400			2150		
MANIF. PRESS.	SUPER-CHARGER	FUEL Gal/Min	MANIF. PRESS.	SUPER-CHARGER	FUEL Gal/Min	STD. TEMP. °C	PRESSURE ALTITUDE	STD. TEMP. °F	MANIF. PRESS.	SUPER-CHARGER	FUEL GPH	MANIF. PRESS.	SUPER-CHARGER	FUEL GPH
						-55.0	40,000 FT.	-67.0						
						-55.0	38,000 FT.	-67.0						
						-55.0	36,000 FT.	-67.0						
						-52.4	34,000 FT.	-62.3						
						-48.4	32,000 FT.	-55.1						
						-44.4	30,000 FT.	-48.0						
						-40.5	28,000 FT.	-40.9						
						-36.5	26,000 FT.	-33.7					F.T.	HIGH	66
						-32.5	24,000 FT.	-26.5				F.T.	"	80
						-28.6	22,000 FT.	-19.4				28	"	82
						-24.6	20,000 FT.	-12.3	F.T.	HIGH	156	28	"	78
			F.T.	HIGH		-20.7	18,000 FT.	-5.2	F.T.	"	174	28	"	75
			43.5	"		-16.7	16,000 FT.	2.0	39.5	"	168	F.T.	LOW	84
			43.5	"		-12.7	14,000 FT.	9.1	39.5	"	162	F.T.	"	90
			43.5	"		-8.8	12,000 FT.	15.2	39.5	"	160	F.T.	"	104
			F.T.	LOW	3.2	-4.8	10,000 FT.	23.4	F.T.	LOW	170	31	"	105
			F.T.	"	3.4	-0.8	8,000 FT.	30.5	F.T.	"	180	31	"	96
			F.T.	"	3.5	3.1	6,000 FT.	37.6	F.T.	"	187	31	"	88
			43.5	"	3.7	7.1	4,000 FT.	44.7	41	"	192	31	"	82
			43.5	"	3.5	11.0	2,000 FT.	51.8	41	"	187	31	"	78
			43.5	"	3.4	15.0	SEA LEVEL	59.0	41	"	182	31	"	74

GENERAL NOTES

(1) OIL CONSUMPTION: MAXIMUM U.S. QUART PER HOUR PER ENGINE
(2) Gal/Min: APPROXIMATE U.S. GALLON PER MINUTE PER ENGINE
(3) GPH: APPROXIMATE U.S. GALLON PER HOUR PER ENGINE.
F.T.: MEANS FULL THROTTLE OPERATION.
VALUES ARE FOR LEVEL FLIGHT WITH RAM.

FOR COMPLETE CRUISING DATA SEE APPENDIX II
NOTE: TO DETERMINE CONSUMPTION IN BRITISH IMPERIAL UNITS, MULTIPLY BY 10 THEN DIVIDE BY 12. RED FIGURES ARE PRELIMINARY SUBJECT TO REVISION AFTER FLIGHT CHECK.

TAKE-OFF CONDITIONS: 2800 RPM, 49 IN. HG., AUTO RICH, LOW BLOWER, DIRECT AIR, **5 MIN.** 263 C, MAX. CYL. TEMP.	CONDITIONS TO AVOID:

SPECIAL NOTES

USE AUTO RICH MIXTURE FOR ALL GROUND OPERATION, TAKE-OFF, LANDING AND LANDING APPROACH, AND WHEN COOLING IS INADEQUATE IN AUTO LEAN. USE AUTO LEAN AT ALL POWERS IN FLIGHT PROVIDED CYLINDER HEAD TEMPERATURE LIMITS ARE NOT EXCEEDED.

SHIFT TO HIGH BLOWER AT MILITARY POWER AT THE ALTITUDE WHERE THE MANIFOLD PRESSURE DROPS TO 34 INCHES IN LOW BLOWER.

SHIFT TO HIGH BLOWER AT NORMAL RATED POWER AT THE ALTITUDE WHEN THE MANIFOLD PRESSURE DROPS TO 32 INCHES IN LOW BLOWER.

AT MAXIMUM CRUISE AND LOWER POWERS SHIFT AT 16,000 FEET PRESSURE ALTITUDE.
* 248°C permissible for 1 hr. with AUTO RICH mixture.
DATA AS OF 6-1-45 BASED ON FIG. 87, ENGINE CALIBRATION CURVE.

Figure 48 — Power Plant Chart

Section III

AN 01-190EB-1

2. AIR SPEED INSTALLATION CORRECTION.

The calibration below represents the air speed head (Pitot Tube) position error and gives the corrected indicated air speed for a given reading of the cockpit air speed indicator, assuming zero scale error for the instrument itself.

AIRSPEED INSTALLATION CORRECTION TABLE	
INDICATED AIR SPEED	CORRECTION
FLAPS AND LANDING GEAR RETRACTED	
100 KNOTS (115 m.p.h.)	SUBTRACT 4 KNOTS (4.6 m.p.h.)
140 KNOTS (161 m.p.h.)	SUBTRACT 3 KNOTS (3.5 m.p.h.)
180 KNOTS (208 m.p.h.)	SUBTRACT 2 KNOTS (2.3 m.p.h.)
220 KNOTS (254 m.p.h.)	SUBTRACT 1 KNOT (1.2 m.p.h.)
FLAPS AND LANDING GEAR EXTENDED	
70 KNOTS (81 m.p.h.)	SUBTRACT 6 KNOTS (6.9 m.p.h.)
80 KNOTS (92 m.p.h.)	SUBTRACT 6 KNOTS (6.9 m.p.h.)
90 KNOTS (104 m.p.h.)	SUBTRACT 4 KNOTS (4.6 m.p.h.)
100 KNOTS (115 m.p.h.)	SUBTRACT 4 KNOTS (4.6 m.p.h.)
110 KNOTS (127 m.p.h.)	SUBTRACT 3 KNOTS (3.5 m.p.h.)

Figure 49 — Airspeed Installation Correction Table

SECTION IV
EMERGENCY OPERATIONS

1. POWER PLANT FAILURE AND EMERGENCY OPERATION.

a. EMERGENCY STARTING.—When the batteries are low and battery carts are not available, start the engine manually by using the starter crank and gear box. The starter crank and gear box are stowed under the bombardier's door.

b. EMERGENCY TAKE-OFF.—Start the engine in the normal manner, then if the engine oil was properly diluted when the engine was previously stopped, the oil pressure should quickly steady itself within the limits set forth in the Power Plant Chart in Section III. If the oil pressure is too high, fluctuates or falls back when the engine R.P.M. is increased, the oil dilution toggle switch may be moved to the ON position for intervals of a few seconds over a period of about fifteen seconds. The oil pressure gage should be watched carefully as over-dilution and low oil pressure is likely to result under these conditions. The airplane may be flown as soon as the oil temperature is 20°C (68°F), the oil pressure is steady, the engine is running smoothly and will take the throttle.

c. GENERATOR FAILURE.

(1) VOLTAGE TOO HIGH. - Turn generator switch off and reduce load on battery to minimum. Recharge battery from time to time by turning generator switch on for five minutes.

(2) VOLTAGE TOO LOW. - If the voltmeter reading falls as low as 24.0 volts during flight, check the operation of the generator system as directed in NOTE, paragraph 6.h. of Section II. If the generator proves to be inoperative, turn off all but the most essential electrical equipment.

d. EMERGENCY OPERATION OF ELECTRICAL SYSTEM.—In the case of generator failure, shut off all unnecessary electrical equipment and land as soon as possible. In the case of a circuit failure, push the circuit breakers reset button, located on the pilot's electrical distribution panel to reset the circuit. If failure is momentary, resetting of circuit breaker button will return circuit to operation.

d. POWER PLANT FAILURE IN FLIGHT.

(1) Put the nose down and maintain flying speed.

(2) If there is time, check the following possible causes of engine failure:

(*a*) Fuel tank may be dry—try shifting to another tank.

(*b*) Fuel pressure may have dropped—use electric fuel pump.

(*c*) Mixture control may have slipped—tighten friction crab and reset control.

(*d*) Ignition may be on one magneto only—move switch to both.

(3) If the engine cannot be restarted, lower the wing flaps to the full "DOWN" position.

(4) If there is time and the airplane is carrying bombs or a torpedo, open bomb bay doors and drop the bombs or the torpedo. If droppable gasoline tanks are carried, drop them also, then *close bomb bay doors.*

(5) Turn ignition switch OFF.

(6) If a suitable airfield is available, the landing gear may be lowered. If not, leave landing gear up.

(7) Turn battery switch OFF.

(8) Land straight ahead.

e. FIRE.—There is no fire extinguisher furnished in this airplane.

2. HYDRAULIC SYSTEM FAILURE.

a. In the event of complete failure of the hydraulic system, the landing gear can be lowered by pulling the landing gear emergency release "T" handle located directly below the hydraulic control. The weight of the landing gear and the action of the springs in the actuating cylinders will cause the wheels to drop and lock in the full down position.

b. Reduce airspeed to 95 knots (110 mph) or less before pulling the emergency release.

c. Lock handle into place by rotating it 45 degrees clockwise.

d. If wheels do not drop immediately, relieve pressure on landing gear hooks by attempting to raise the landing gear hydraulically or applying a negative gravity maneuver while pulling out the emergency release handle.

e. The wing flaps are not equipped with locks for holding them in the DOWN position, but depend on the hydraulic pressure in the wing flap actuating cylinders remaining constant. If there is a leak in the circuit, the slip stream may force the flaps UP. If it is felt that all the available pressure will be needed to lower the flaps and keep them down while landing, use the emergency "T" handle to lower the landing gear and this will avoid using up the reserve supply of pressure in the accumulator, which is normally sufficient to operate the wing flap cylinders and hold the flaps DOWN.

f. After landing, find the cause of the hydraulic failure, restore hydraulic system to normal operation and return the emergency release handle to its normal position.

3. DITCHING.

This airplane should have good water landing characteristics. Actual water landings indicate that the

Section IV
Paragraph 3, 4   AN 01-190EB-1

airplane will remain afloat for approximately 15 to 20 seconds under the following conditions:

   a. Bomb Bay load dropped if possible.
   b. Bomb Bay doors closed.
   c. Wheels up.
   d. Flaps down.
   e. Fully stalled—power stall if power is available.

If altitude does not permit emptying the bomb bay and closing the doors, it may be preferable to land with the doors closed. The bomber's window would probably be broken and the bomber's compartment immediately filled if a landing is made with the bomb bay doors open. Water landing with Landing Gear extended and bomb bay doors open may cause the airplane to dive.

4. LIFE RAFT.

   a. GENERAL.

(1) A Mark 4, Type "D" droppable life raft is stowed in a compartment, extending through the upper part of the fuselage, between the middle compartment and the turret. The compartment has doors on both the port and starboard sides of the fuselage.

The life raft is equipped with a CO_2 cylinder for inflation, an emergency equipment container, an oar pocket, a supply pocket and a repair pocket, which contain the following equipment.

   (*a*) EMERGENCY EQUIPMENT CONTAINER.
     1. One first aid kit.
     2. Emergency rations (one package per man).
     3. Emergency drinking water (two cans per man).
     4. One sea marker.
     5. Two M-8 smoke grenades.

   (*b*) OAR POCKET.
     1. Two five-foot oars.
     2. One emergency hand pump.
     3. Two sails.
     4. Smoke grenade holding clamp.

   (*c*) SUPPLY POCKET.
     1. Fishing kit.
     2. Match container compass.
     3. Two smoke grenades.
     4. One knife.
     5. Twenty-five feet of cord.
     6. One chromium-plated reflector disc.
     7. Life raft fish spear.

(d) REPAIR POCKET.
 1. Rubber Cement.
 2. Tire patches.
 3. Patching material.
 4. Roughing tool.
 5. Pliers.
 6. Scissors.
 7. Leak plugs.

b. REMOVAL.—Either door may be removed by releasing the two quick release latches at the bottom of the door. Pull the life raft out of the compartment.

c. INFLATION.—The life raft is packed in a carrying case equipped with quick opening devices. When the CO_2 gas is discharged into the buoyant chambers the life raft will emerge and fall free of the container. The raft is so packed, that a hand grip for the manual operation of the gas discharge is readily accessible.

Figure 50 — Pilot's Compartment Emergency Release

5. EMERGENCY EXITS.

a. PILOT'S COMPARTMENT.—Pull INBOARD on the Red Painted Release Lever on the Left Side Panel—PUSH the panel OUT.

Figure 51 — Bombardier's Compartment Emergency Release

Figure 52 — Turret Emergency Release

b. MIDDLE COMPARTMENT.—Pull INBOARD on the Red Painted Knob on the right side—then rotate handle and PUSH UP on the enclosure.

c. BOMBARDIER'S COMPARTMENT.—Pull UP on the Red Painted Lever just forward of the door. This pulls out the door hinge pins, and the door can then be pushed out and jettisoned.

d. TURRET.—In case of crash landing or ditching, or for quick exit in some other emergency, PUSH the handle at the gunner's right side AFT and push the circular hatch OUTBOARD.

This exit cannot be used in flight, because the gunner does not wear his parachute attached.

Provisions are made for stowing the turret gunner's parachute above the door in the bombardier's compartment.

AN 01-190EB-1

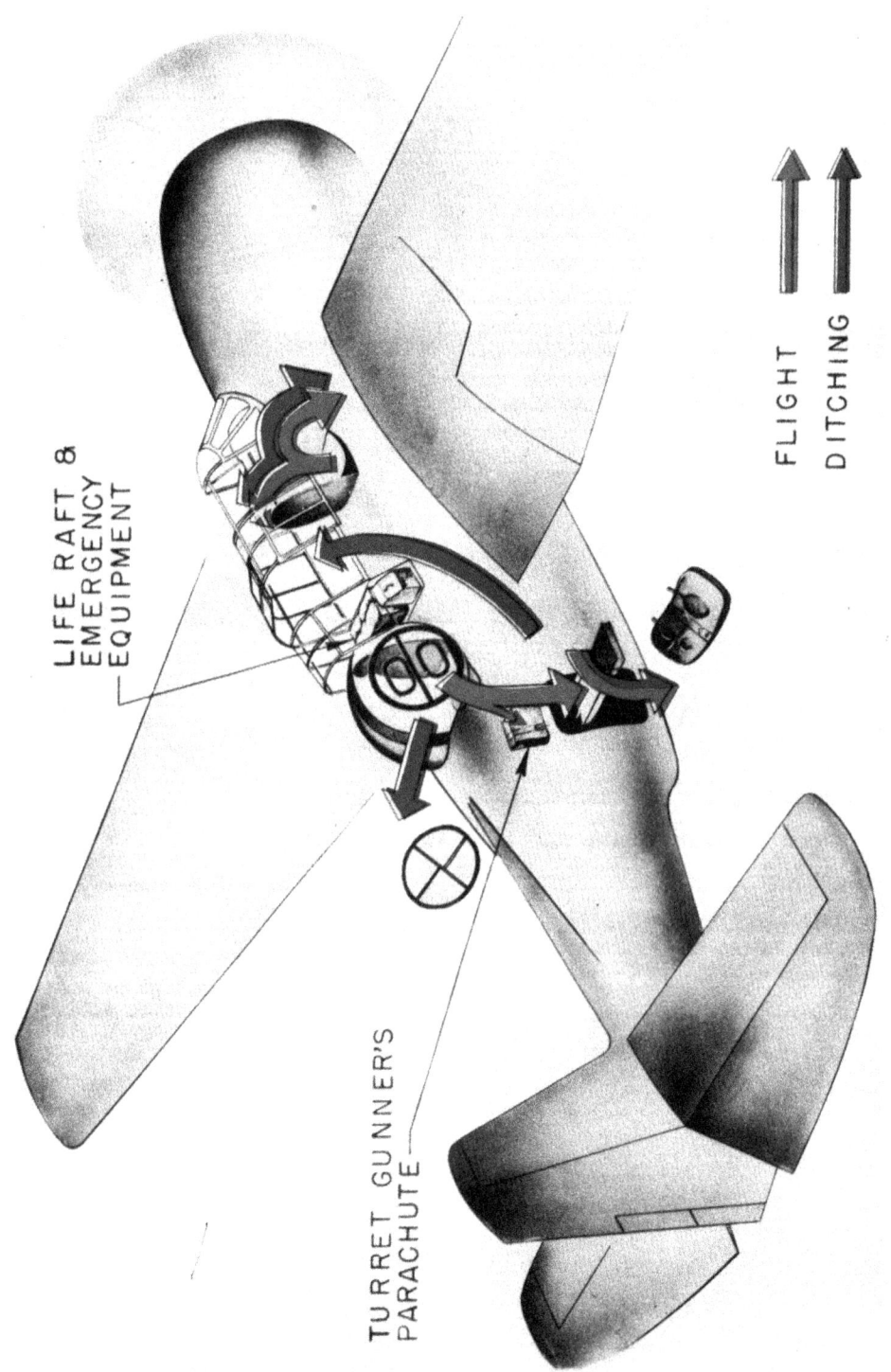

Figure 53 — Emergency Equipment and Exits

Section V
Paragraph 1

AN 01-190EB-1

SECTION V

OPERATIONAL EQUIPMENT

1. MIDDLE COMPARTMENT.

a. GENERAL.—The middle compartment is the area between the pilot's cockpit and the gun turret. In it is installed the following equipment, operated by remote controls.

1. AN/APN-1 Equipment
2. Automatic Pilot Equipment
3. IFF Equipment
4. Oxygen Cylinder
5. AN/ARC-1, VHF Transmitter and Receiver Equipment

(1) The AN/APN-1 Radio Equipment is housed within the upper part of the turnover structure.

(2) The AN/ARC-1 Transmitter-Receiver equipment is mounted on a shelf, hinged to the port side of the fuselage.

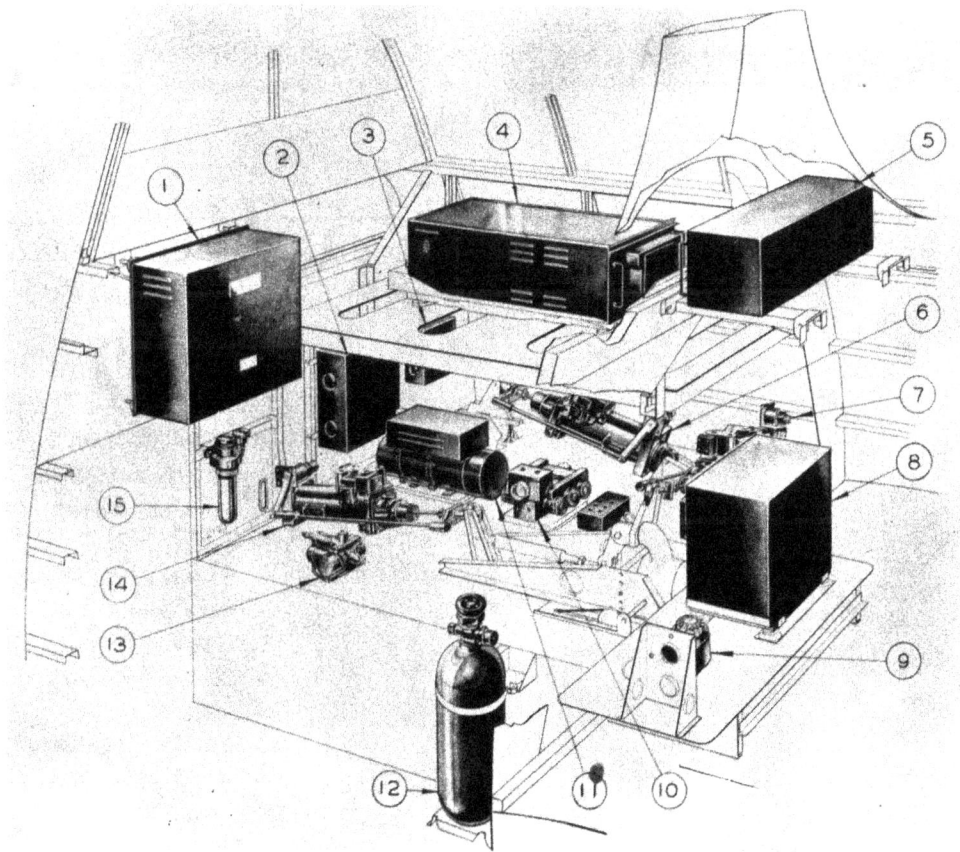

1 Auto Pilot Servo Amplifier	6 Rudder Servo Unit	11 Inverter
2 Auto Pilot Junction Box	7 Aileron Servo Unit	12 Oxygen Bottle
3 Second Cockpit Radio Power Box	8 AN/APX-2 Transmitter-Receiver	13 Auto Pilot Pressure Regulator
4 AN/ARC-1 Transmitter-Receiver	9 Impact Switch	14 Elevator Servo
5 AN/APN-1 Transmitter-Receiver	10 Transfer Valve	15 Auto Pilot Oil Filter

Figure 54 — Middle Compartment

(3) The Automatic Pilot Equipment is installed directly under the aforementioned shelf which extends from the turnover structure to the bombardier's compartment, and controlled by the pilot.

(4) The Oxygen Supply Cylinder is located in the passageway on the starboard side of the middle compartment with tubes leading to the pilot's compartment and to two stations in the bombardier's compartment. There is a control valve at the cylinder and flow control valves at each of the three stations.

(5) In airplanes Serial Nos. 22857 to 23313 inclusive two gasoline heaters, installed on the starboard side of the passage way to the second cockpit forward of the bombardier's compartment, furnish heat for the pilot's and bombardier's compartments. The control switch for one is on the pilot's distribution panel and the other on the bombardier's control panel. Airplanes Serial Nos. 23314 to 23656, 68062 to 69538, 85459 to 85780 inclusive are furnished with one heater for pilot's cockpit heating and windshield defrosting. No heaters are furnished in airplanes Serial No. 85781 and subsequent.

2. BOMBARDIER'S COMPARTMENT.

a. GENERAL.—The bombardier's compartment extends from the turret to the rear of the fuselage. This compartment has provisions for carrying one of the airplane's crew members, the radar man-bombardier. A seat, hinged to the fuselage structure on the port side of the compartment, can be lowered into position or raised to accommodate the radar man-bombardier.

The compartment is accessible through a door on the right side of the fuselage. Windows on both sides and the rear of the compartment afford vision to the exterior. An instrument panel with an inclinometer, altimeter and outside air temperature gage is located at the front port side of the compartment.

b. OXYGEN EQUIPMENT.—An oxygen regulator is provided for the bombardier-radar man.

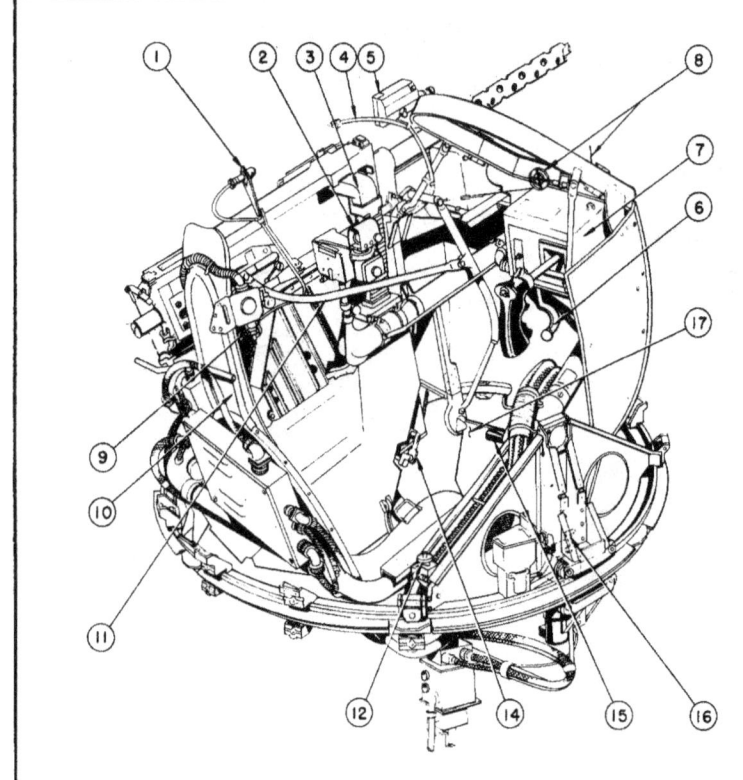

1. Light
2. Illuminated Gun Sight
3. Link Ejection Chute
4. Solenoid Conduit
5. Gun Camera
6. Manual Firing Trigger
7. Main Control Unit
8. Ring and Bead Gun Sights
9. Oxygen Regulator
10. Seat
11. Gun Charging Lever
12. Manual Train Clutch
14. Manual Elevation Crank
15. Manual Train Crank
16. Electric Train Clutch
17. Moveable Armor Plate

Figure 55 — Turret

c. RADIO AND COMMUNICATIONS.—(See paragraph 6.).

d. BOMBING EQUIPMENT.—(See paragraph 8.)

3. TURRET.

a. GENERAL.—The electrically operated gun turret is located in the top of the fuselage, just aft of the hooded enclosure of the second compartment. The turret is equipped with a .50 caliber automatic machine gun, with container for 200 rounds of ammunition, an illuminated gun sight, a gun camera, an oxygen regulator and flow indicator, radio control box and light.

The control provided for the operation of the turret is designed to give normal speed in both elevation and train or a higher speed for slewing. The normal elevation speed is 12° per second and the normal train speed is 20° per second. The high speed switch, on the control unit, increases the speed to 30° per second for elevation and 45° per second for train operation. The vertical motion has a range of 115°, 30° below to 85° above the horizontal and the train motion operates either clockwise or counterclockwise through 360°

b. ELECTRICAL CONTROLS.

(1) MAIN CONTROL UNIT.—This unit, located directly in front of the gunner, controls and directs the movement of the turret and the firing of the gun. It contains the Master Power Switch and a movable pistol grip control handle. (Fig. 56)

(a) MASTER POWER SWITCH.—The turret's electrical system is energized when the Master Power Switch is in the ON position.

(b) CONTROL HANDLE.—The pistol grip control handle has incorporated in it the Action Switch, the High Speed Switch and the trigger for electrically firing the machine gun.

The action switch, on the lower front of the control handle, must be held closed, to make the turret controls operative. When the Action Switch is released, the turret automatically returns to its neutral position with the gun muzzle trailing aft and the electrical power to the motors cut off. In returning to the neutral position, the turret first returns in train to neutral by the shortest path, then the elevation returns to neutral. These functions do not occur simultaneously, but in the sequence given. Both the train and elevation drive units are equipped with automatic cut-

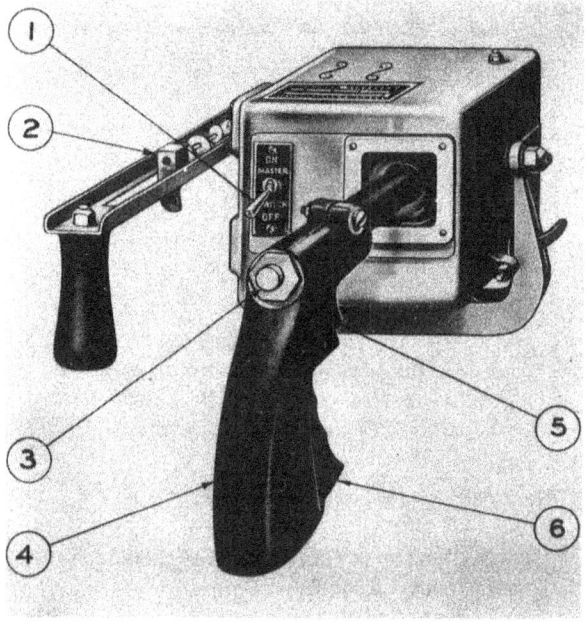

1. Master Switch
2. Manual Gun Trigger
3. Slewing Switch
4. Control Handle
5. Electrical Gun Trigger
6. Action Switch

Figure 56 — Turret Main Control Unit

out switches, so that in case of failure in one motion, either train or elevation, the remaining motion may be controlled electrically.

The High Speed Switch located on the rear of the control handle is for slewing only.

(2) SWITCH BOX AND SWITCHES.—The elevation switch, the train power switch and the gun firing switch, located on the switch box, at the gunner's left shoulder, must be turned ON before the turret can be operated. Also mounted on the switch box is the light switch and a receptacle for the illuminated gun sight connection. (Fig. 57).

(3) EMERGENCY SWITCH.—This switch is located on the port side of the bombardier's compartment. It is equipped with a circuit breaker reset button. The Emergency Switch is normally "closed" and the junction box cover must be removed to open the circuit and so cut off power to the turret.

Section V
Paragraph 3, 4
AN 01-190EB-1

1. Illuminated Gun Sight Receptacle
2. Firing Circuit Reset Button
3. Train Switch
4. Elevation Switch
5. Light Switch

Figure 57 — Turret Switch Box and Switches

c. MANUAL OPERATING EQUIPMENT.

(1) CLUTCH LEVER.—This lever is on the top of the train motor, at the lower right side of the turret gunner. The turret may be rotated freely, with the clutch disengaged.

To engage clutch, pull lever UP. To disengage clutch, push lever DOWN.

(2) MANUAL ELEVATION CRANK. — The crank for manual elevation is at the left of the gunner, just below the gun charging handle. The turret can be elevated by rotating the crank clockwise and depressed by rotating the crank counterclockwise.

Note

Partially unfold the handle and rotate until the clutch engages, then completely unfold the handle and operate as desired.

(3) MANUAL TRAIN DRIVE.—The crank handle for manual train operation is stowed on the armor plate at the gunner's right. To operate the manual train drive, remove the crank handle and engage it with the crank shaft. Disengage the electric train clutch located to the front of the gunner by pushing it down and engage the manual train clutch located to the right of the gunner by turning the knob counterclockwise. Turn the handle in the direction of resultant action desired, clockwise rotates the turret to the gunner's left, counterclockwise to the gunner's right.

d. OPERATION.

(1) Lock the hinged armor plate in the UP position.

(2) Move the Elevation Power Switch, located on the junction box, to the ON position.

(3) Move the Train Power Switch, located on the same box, to the ON position.

(4) Move the Main Power Switch, on the control box, to ON.

(5) Squeeze the Action Switch, on the pistol grip handle, with the lower two fingers.

(6) Point the Main Control Grip in the direction desired and the turret will follow.

(7) If higher speed is desired, press the High Speed Switch, on the rear of the pistol grip, with the thumb.

(8) If the turret stops due to an overload, open the Master Switch and wait for at least 30 seconds. The cut-out switches on the switch box should be set to the OFF position and then turned to ON. Power may again be applied to the amplidyne motor-generator by closing the Master Switch and the Action Switch.

WARNING

Keep hands and feet clear of the moving parts of the turret.

4. OXYGEN SYSTEM.

a. GENERAL. (Fig. 59)—A high pressure, diluter-demand type oxygen system is provided in the airplane. The oxygen cylinder and its filler plug are located on the starboard side of the middle compartment. The cylinder contains 514 cu. inches of oxygen under a pressure of 1800 p.s.i. plus or minus 50 p.s.i. Each member has a separate diluter-demand regulator and oxygen flow indicator at his station. The members of the crew have access to oxygen at all times while in flight.

The system is designed to meet the demands of each individual at all altitudes and deliver a properly proportioned mixture of air and oxygen. With the air valve set to the ON or NORMAL OXYGEN position, air is drawn into the breathing system and is automatically mixed with oxygen from the supply cylinder. Beyond 30,000 ft. altitude, 100% cylinder oxygen is delivered. With the air valve set to the "OFF" or "100% OXYGEN" position, 100% oxygen is delivered at all altitudes.

The diluter-demand regulator (Fig. 58) for each member may be adjusted while performing his duties in flight. The pilot's regulator is fixed on the starboard side of the armor plate aft of the pilot's seat. The bombardier's regulator is located on the port side of the bombardier's compartment just above the seat and the regulator for the turret gunner is rigidly attached within the revolving turret. If the turret gunner is in the bombardier's compartment acting as the radioman he must operate his regulator by reaching up into the turret.

If the regulator at any station fails to function properly, an emergency valve on the regulator can be turned ON. With the emergency valve turned to the ON position a flow of 100% oxygen will be delivered to the mask.

Figure 58 — Oxygen Regulator

b. PRE-FLIGHT CHECK.—Prior to any flight in which oxygen is to be used or is likely to be used, the following items should be checked, to assure proper functioning of the oxygen system.

(1) Make certain the emergency valves are OFF.

(2) Open the cylinder valve and allow at least 10 seconds for the pressure in the line to equalize. The pressure gage should read approximately 1800 p.s.i. if the cylinder is fully charged.

(3) Close the cylinder valve. After a few minutes, observe the pressure gage and simultaneously open the cylinder valve. If the gage pointer jumps, leakage is indicated.

(*a*) If leakage is found, a further test is needed. Open the cylinder valve, carefully noting the pressure gage reading, and then close the cylinder valve. If the gage pointer drops more than 100 p.s.i., in five minutes, there is excessive leakage which must be repaired prior to use.

(4) Check the mask fit by placing the thumb over the end of the mask tube and inhale lightly. If there is no leakage, the mask will adhere tightly to the face, due to the suction created. If the mask leaks, tighten the mask suspension straps and adjust the nose wire. DO NOT USE A MASK THAT LEAKS.

(5) Couple the mask securely to the breathing tube by means of the quick disconnect coupling.

WARNING

The mating parts of the coupling must not be "cocked", but must be fully engaged.

(6) Depress the diaphragm knob through the hole in the center of the regulator case and feel the flow of oxygen into the mask, then release the diaphragm knob.

Note

Since the amount of added oxygen is very small at sea level, the oxygen flow meter may not operate while the plane is on the ground. In this case turn the air valve to OFF or 100% OXYGEN and test again. If the oxygen flow indicator operation is satisfactory, reset the air valve to ON or NORMAL OXYGEN in which setting adequate oxygen flow and BLINKER operation will be assured at oxygen use altitudes.

(7) Check the emergency valve by turning counterclockwise slowly until the oxygen flows vigorously into the mask, then close the emergency valve.

c. OPERATING INSTRUCTIONS.

(1) Open the oxygen cylinder valve. If the cylinder is fully charged, the pressure gage should read approximately 1800 p.s.i. The oxygen cylinder should be opened before take-off, but it may be opened in flight by one of the crew members other than the pilot. Access to the cylinder during flight is from the bombardier's compartment through the passage along the starboard side of the fuselage.

(2) Set the air-valve to ON or NORMAL OXYGEN except when the presence of excessive carbon-monoxide is suspected. In this case set to OFF or 100% OXYGEN.

(3) Put the oxygen mask hose on the regulator and be sure that the quick disconnect coupling is fully engaged.

(4) Check the mask fit frequently while in use.

CAUTION

Never check the mask fit by squeezing the mask tube while the "Emergency" valve is ON.

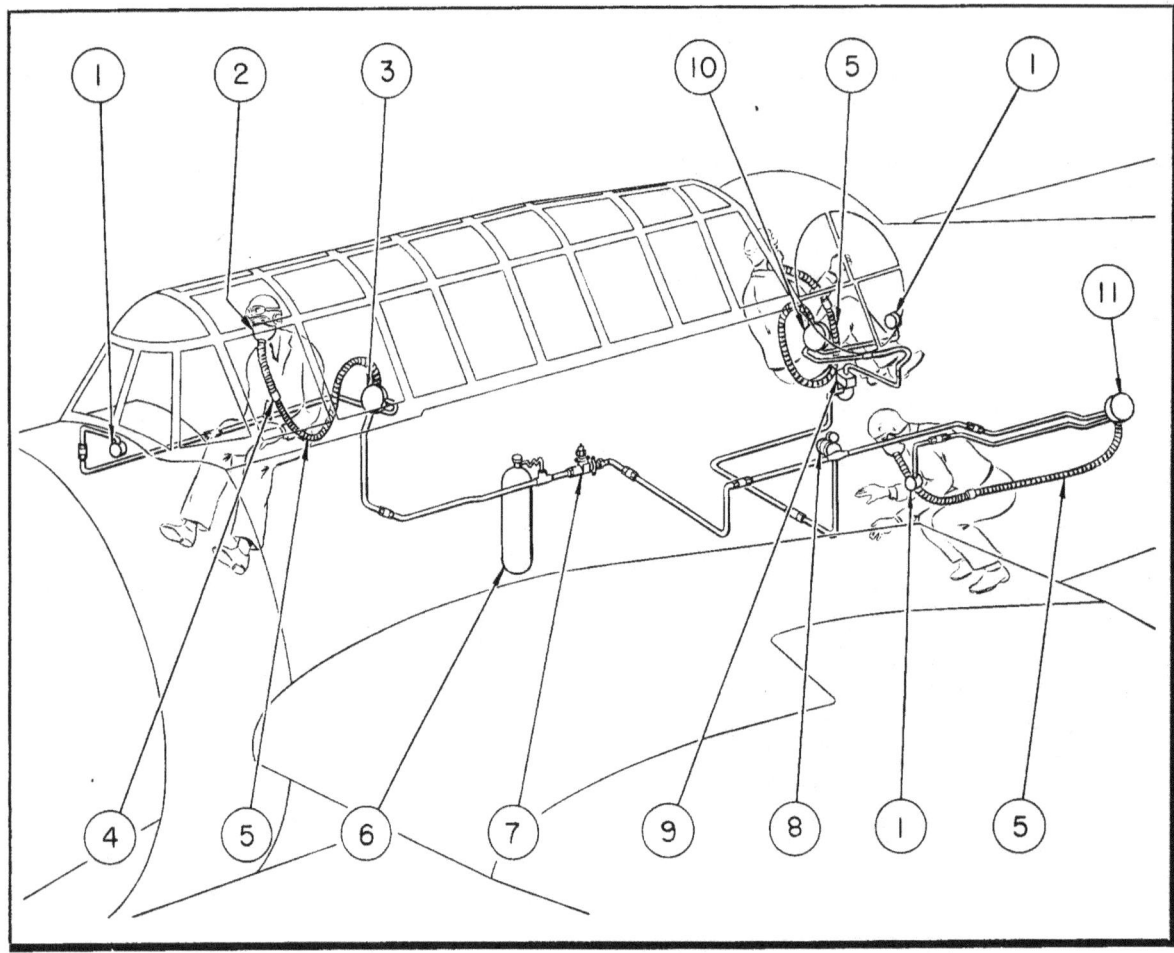

1. Oxygen Flow Indicator
2. Oxygen Mask and Mask Microphone
3. Pilot's Regulator
4. Quick Disconnect Coupling
5. Breathing Tube
6. Oxygen Bottle
7. Filler Assembly
8. Pressure Reducer
9. Oxygen Swivel Joint
10. Turret Gunner's Regulator
11. Bombardier's Regulator

Figure 59 — Oxygen System

(5) Breathe normally and observe the oxygen flow indicator for "blink", verifying positive flow of oxygen.

(6) Frequently check the cylinder pressure gage for state of available oxygen supply, and the oxygen flow indicator for the flow of oxygen to the mask.

(7) Close the cylinder valve on completion of flight.

5. ARMAMENT.

a. GENERAL.—The airplane is equipped with three .50 caliber machine guns. The turret is equipped with one .50 caliber gun which can be fired as the turret is operated. One .50 caliber gun is mounted in a fixed position within each outer panel of the wing.

All ammunition boxes are loaded prior to flight. The turret gun ammunition supply can be replenished during flight.

The wing guns are loaded prior to flight and can be charged at any time by the pilot. Wing guns should not be charged until after take-off and should be in the safe position when landing.

The wing guns hydraulic charger handle protrudes through an opening in the pilot's starboard instrument panel. In later model TBM-3 airplanes the gun charger is located on the shelf to the left of the pilot.

It is recommended that the turret gun should not be loaded or charged until a safe altitude has been reached and that it be unloaded prior to landing.

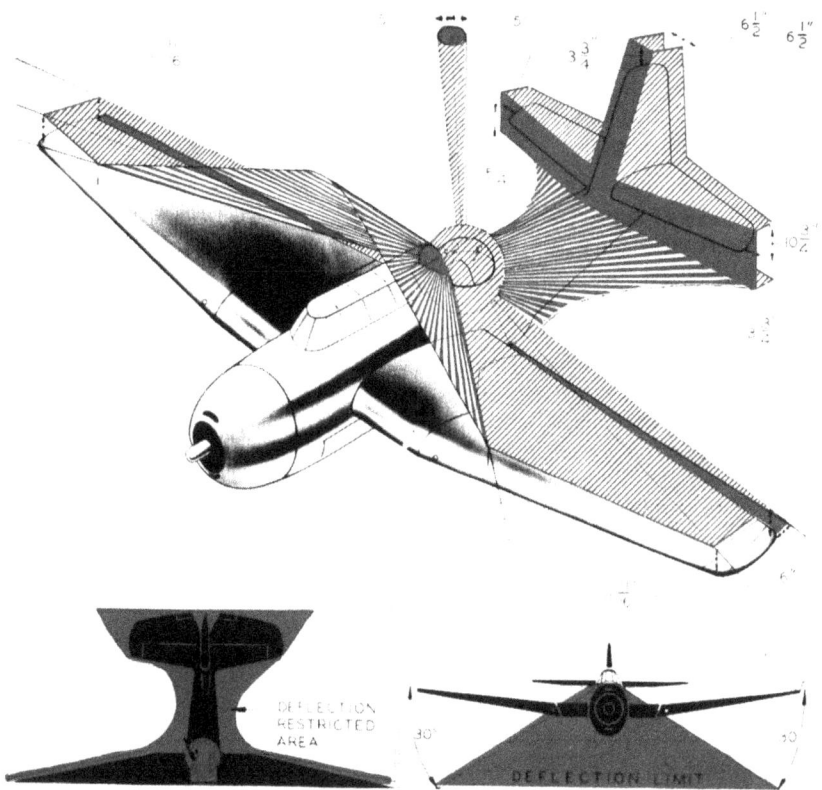

Figure 60 — Angles of Gunfire

The angles of gunfire are shown in figure 60.

Interrupter cams actuate a micro switch in the gun firing circuit automatically stop the firing of the turret gun when the tail and wing surfaces are in line of fire. No interrupters are provided for the pitot tube or antennae.

A track around the circumference of the turret is shaped to follow the contour of the fuselage. A movable arm which is electrically connected to the main turret control switch will ride on the track, when the gun is depressed, automatically limiting the angle of depression of the gun as the turret revolves.

WARNING

No fire interruption is provided when the turret gun is fired manually, consequently the gunner must exercise care in pointing the gun so as not to fire into tail and wing surfaces. Prior to landing the gun charging handle should be pulled to its aft position and locked to preclude the possibility of accidental discharge of the gun.

b. RUNAWAY GUNS.

(1) It is possible due to the wear or deformation of the sear notch or the firing pin extension pin or a weak sear spring for a gun to continue firing after the trigger or trigger switch has been released.

(2) WING GUNS.—To stop a runaway wing gun place the wing gun charger handle in Safe position and charge the guns.

(3) TURRET GUN.—To stop a runaway turret gun pull the manual charging handle to the charge position and lock it.

c. TURRET GUN.

(1) The .50 caliber turret gun is electrically fired by a solenoid on the port side of the gun. An ammunition container of 200 rounds capacity is located on the port side of the gun mount. This container may be replaced by a second container while the airplane is in flight. A second container with an additional 200 rounds is mounted on the starboard side of the bombardier's compartment. There are holes in the

containers with adjacent numbers to indicate the amount of ammunition remaining. The feed chute, on the port side of the gun, has a built-in non-return spring loaded latch which prevents the belt of ammunition from falling back into the feed chute. Links and cases are ejected into a container below the gun.

(2) LOADING AND CHARGING.

WARNING

When raising the cover of the turret gun be careful to keep fingers clear, to avoid injury. There is very little clearance between the end of cover and turret enclosure when cover is fully open.

(*a*) Open the feed chute cover on the port side of the gun and insert the double loop end of the belt through the mouth of the feed chute into the receiver, until the first cartridge is beyond the belt holding pawl.

(*b*) Close the gun cover and the feed chute cover.

(*c*) Pull the charging handle completely to the rear, release it, and allow it to spring forward. Repeat this operation. It is necessary to operate the charging handle twice to get the first cartridge into the chamber and ready to fire.

(3) REPLENISHING AMMUNITION.

(*a*) The ammunition container may be replaced after the initial supply (200 rounds) is exhausted.

(*b*) Move the turret to stowed position with the gun pointing toward the rudder.

(*c*) Release the restricting cable hook from lower edge of box.

(*d*) Pull the YELLOW knob outward. This knob is below the gunsight bracket.

WARNING

The ammunition container must be held from below before the release knob is pulled.

(*e*) The container is now free to be removed, however, it must be held from below so that it will not drop and damage the airplane or equipment.

(*f*) When the loaded container is pushed to the top, locks automatically engage, holding it in place.

(*g*) Fasten cable hook to the lower edge of container.

(*h*) Empty the case and link container whenever ammunition is replenished.

(4) REPLENISHING AMMUNITION, ALTERNATE METHOD.

(*a*) The ammunition may be replenished in rough weather or during evasive tactics with a belt of 180 rounds.

(*b*) The bombardier passes the single loop end of the belt to the turret gunner who feeds it over the top of the gun through the feed chute, into the container, loading the last cartridge into the gun. This method is faster and may be done with the turret in any position.

(5) FIRING.

(*a*) The gun is fired by pressing the trigger switch on the main control grip handle.

(*b*) An alternate manual trigger is located to the port of the main control grip handle. Later models incorporate a pedal trigger in place of the manual trigger.

Note

The ejected links will accumulate where they enter the container if all the firing is done with the gun in a horizontal or depressed position. This will cause stoppage with 10 to 65 rounds unfired. A few bursts with the gun elevated at least 60° before 100 rounds have been fired will prevent this.

(6) SAFETY LATCH.

(*a*) Push the safety latch on the rear of the gun to STARBOARD for safe, PORT for firing.

(*b*) There is an additional safety latch on the gun charger track. Pull the handle back and engage it with the latch. This will render the gun inoperative when landing with unused ammunition.

(7) UNLOADING.

(*a*) Raise cover, remove belt, retract bolt by pulling back charging handle and by visual inspection make certain that gun is unloaded.

(*b*) Release bolt and close cover.

(*c*) Press trigger to relieve tension on firing pin spring.

d. WING GUNS.

(1) The .50 caliber guns in the wing are hydraulically charged and electrically fired. The ammunition box for each gun is installed in a compartment outboard of the gun and the ammunition belt is guided by a connecting feed chute. The shell cases and links are ejected downward and clear of the lower surface of the wing, through two vertical chutes.

The ammunition load per gun is 280 rounds in the ammunition box and 40 rounds which may be carried in the ammunition feed chute.

(2) CHARGING THE WING GUNS.

(*a*) The gun charging control valve is located on the starboard instrument panel. This valve is designed to charge the guns ready for firing or to hold the action in SAFE position.

(*b*) Turn the hydraulic control valve handle to "Push-to-Charge". The handle will be automatically released on completion of the charging stroke.

(3) FIRING THE WING GUNS.

(*a*) Close the Wing Gun Switch on the pilot's distribution panel.

(b) Close the Armament Master Switch on the pilot's distribution panel.

(c) Press and release the Gun Trigger Switch on the pilot's control column.

WARNING

BEFORE LANDING, THE WING GUN SWITCH AND ARMAMENT MASTER SWITCH MUST BE SWITCHED OFF TO PREVENT ACCIDENTAL DISCHARGE OF THE UNUSED AMMUNITION. THE WARNING HORN WILL EMIT AN INTERMITTENT SIGNAL IF ARMAMENT MASTER SWITCH IS ON AND LANDING GEAR IS LOWERED, IN LATER AIRPLANES.

(4) SAFE CONDITION OF WING GUNS.

(a) To hold the action of the gun in SAFE position, turn the knob to "Push-to-Safe" and push in.

(b) To release the action when in SAFE position, turn the handle to the position "Push-to-Charge".

(5) EMERGENCY CHARGING OF WING GUNS.—When the hydraulic system pressure is below 800 lbs., set the hand pump selector valve on GENERAL and operate the hydraulic hand pump, to build up sufficient pressure to charge guns, and charge as outlined above.

e. GUN SIGHTS AND CAMERAS.

(1) The turret gun is equipped with an illuminated sight. Illumination of the sight is controlled by a thumb screw switch which can be turned to OFF, NIGHT or DAY to allow varying degrees of light to enter the optics of the sight. In the rear of the hooded section of the sight is a smoked glass which may be moved into or out of the line of sight by means of a scalloped thumb wheel control. A spare bulb container including three bulbs is mounted on the sight bracket.

(2) WING GUNS SIGHT.—The Mark 8 illuminated gun sight provided in this airplane is used as the Wing Gun Sight as well as the Bomb and Torpedo Sight. The sight is located in a recess in the cowling forward of the pilot's instrument panel and aft of the windshield. The control panel for the sight is mounted below the pilot's distribution panel. To use the sight set the switch to ON, then turn the rheostat to adjust the intensity of the image. The bulb incorporates two filaments. If the bulb does not illuminate set the switch to ON-ALTERNATE to use the second filament.

An auxiliary ring and bead sight is mounted to the starboard of the Mark 8 sight on earlier model TBM-3 airplanes.

(3) TORPEDO CAMERA.—The torpedo camera is installed under the left wing panel, and is controlled by a switch on the pilot's Electrical Distribution Panel.

(4) GUN CAMERAS.—Provisions are made for mounting Type AN-N6 and AN-N6A Gun Cameras, for use with all guns. The cameras are 35 mm fixed focus type, equipped with a film footage indicator and film speed adjusting knob. The cameras operate at any time the guns are fired, unless electrical connections are disconnected at the cameras.

Figure 61 — Mark 8 Sight

f. GUN PACKAGES.

(1) GENERAL.—Provisions are made for mounting a Douglas Gun Package or a 500 lb. bomb on the under surface of each wing outer panel, just outboard of the R.P. installation. The Radar Bomb is also provided for in this installation and is installed under the starboard panel, when the gun package is not used. The Douglas Gun Package is a compact completely self contained unit, mounting two (2). 50 caliber machine guns with provision for a maximum of 340 rounds of ammunition per gun.

The two guns, spaced $7\frac{1}{2}$ inches apart, mounted in recoil adapters, are located in the forward portion of the package. A 285 round ammunition box is mounted directly behind each gun. An additional 55 rounds per gun may be carried in the flexible feed chutes. Cases and links are ejected through the bottom of the package. An ammunition booster is provided to insure positive feed. Provisions are incorporated in the package for adjusting the guns through a total of (3°) three degrees in elevation and (2°) two degrees in azimuth. The packages are suspended from Mk. 51 bomb racks and may be jettisoned by energizing the bomb release mechanism of the bomb rack. The starboard "T" fittings are mounted on the starboard wing panel of production airplanes together with a Mk. 51 Bomb Rack to accommodate the radar bomb. The port fittings, sway brace assemblies and hardware needed for installation of the gun packages are, however, shipped as loose parts.

(2) OPERATION.— The package guns are charged manually from the deck, or electrically when electric chargers are installed. The Package Guns can be fired simultaneously with the wing guns or independently, by the pilot.

(a) The procedure for firing the Package Guns is as follows:

1. Close the "Container Guns" switch. This switch is located on the pilot's distribution panel.

2. Close the "Armament Master" switch which is also located on the pilot's distribution panel.

3. Press the "Gun Trigger", which is located on the pilot's control stick, to fire guns.

(b) The Gun Package, Wing Bombs, or Radar Unit can be dropped from the airplane by the pilot, who employs the following procedure.

1. Close the "Container Guns—Radar—Wing Bomb Release" switch.

2. Close the "Armament Master" switch.

3. Press and release the "Bomb Release" button which is located on the top aft side of the control stick.

g. R.P. INSTALLATION.

(1) GENERAL.—Provisions are made for the installation of four (4) rocket projectiles under each wing. The rockets are mounted on Mk. 5 Zero Launchers.

The rocket projectiles are fired electrically in pairs, the corresponding projectiles on each wing being fired simultaneously. The electrical controls consist of the bomb release button, which is located on the top, aft, side of the control stick, the Bomb Torpedo R.P. switch on the pilot's distribution panel, and the R.P. Distributor which is mounted on a bracket below the instrument panel. The MK 1 Rocket Selector Switch replaces the R.P. Distributor in later model TBM-3 airplanes. This switch is located on the pilot's lower port instrument panel directly below the ignition switch.

Incorporated in the Distributor, which can be set to control the number of pairs to be fired, is an ON-OFF switch, a removable Safety Plug, a Jewel light which illuminates when the circuit is energized, an Arm-Safe Lever and an Automatic-Select Switch. When the Automatic-Select Switch is on Automatic the selector automatically sets up the circuit for the next station after each pair has been fired; thus any number of pairs from one to four can be fired depending on the selector setting. With the Automatic-Select switch on Select, only one pair of rockets can be fired with each setting of the selector switch.

The MK 1 Rocket Selector Switch permits the pilot to select the number of rockets to be fired and the sequence of firing. The switch selector knob permits selection of the rockets to be fired. Selection is made by turning the knob counterclockwise. The knob cannot be turned clockwise, to return the knob to SALVO depress the salvo preset button located in the center of the selector knob. The selector switch is devised to release the rockets in the following combinations: released in pairs; two the first release, two the second release, four the third release; two the first release, six the second release; and salvo release.

(2) OPERATION.

(a) The pilot employs the following procedure to fire the rocket projectiles in airplanes equipped with the R.P. Distributor.

1. Set the "Bomb Torpedo—R.P." Switch to R.P.

2. Set the On-Off Switch of the Distributor to ON.

Figure 62A — R.P. Distribution Unit (Used on Earlier TBM-3 Airplanes)

Figure 62B — R.P. Selector Switch (Used on Later TBM-3 Airplanes)

3. Move the Automatic-Select Switch to the position desired.

4. If the Automatic-Select Switch has been placed on Automatic and the selector is set on One, the projectiles will be fired at set intervals from Stations one to four consecutively. If set on Two, Stations two, three and four will fire. If set on Three, Stations three and four will fire, while if set on four only number four will fire. If the switch is on Select, the selector switch will have to be set manually to the number corresponding to the next pair to be fired.

5. Insert the safety plug in the Distributor.

Note

The red jewel warning light illuminates showing that the circuit is energized and the system is operative.

6. Push the Arm-Safe switch to Arm.

7. Close the Armament Master switch.

8. Press the Bomb Release Button to fire rocket projectiles.

WARNING

The rocket safety plug should never be inserted in the distributor socket during ground operations. It should be inserted only after take-off and removed prior to landing.

(b) The pilot employs the following procedure to fire the rocket projectiles using the MK 1 selector switch.

1. Set the "Bomb Torpedo R.P." switch to R.P.

2. Set the selector switch to the desired position.

3. Close the R.P. fusing switch.

4. Close the Armament Master switch.

5. Press Bomb Release Button located on the top of the grip of the pilot's control stick to release the rockets.

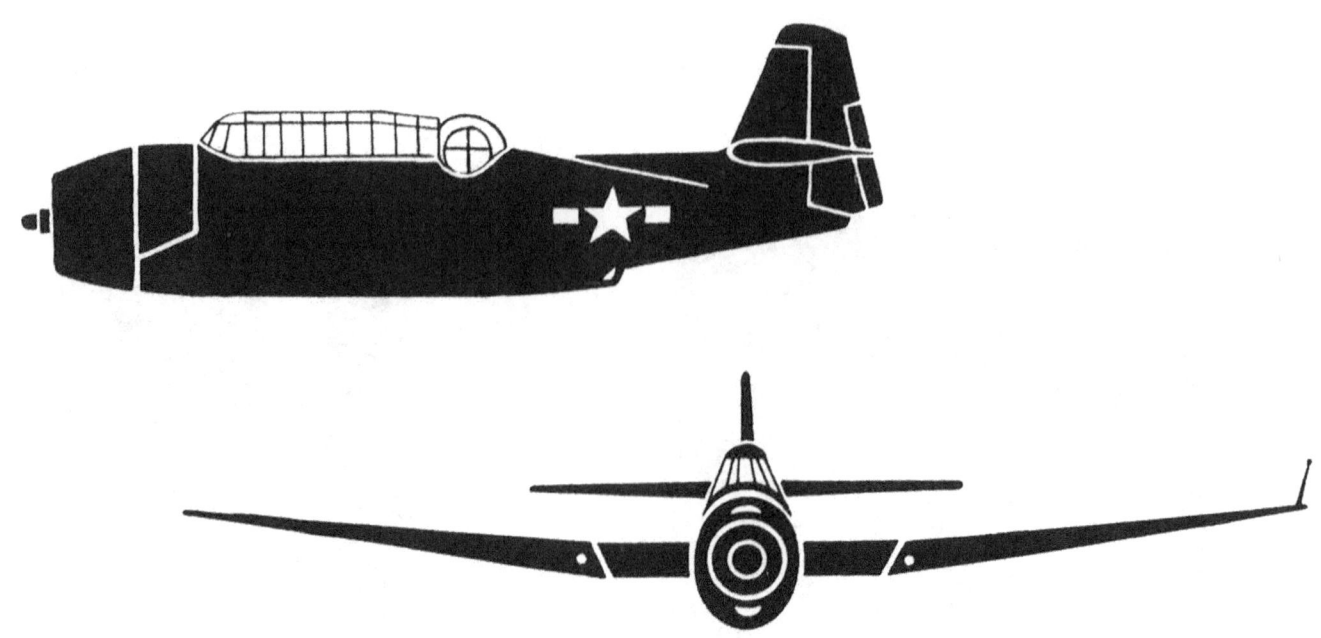

THIS PAGE INTENTIONALLY LEFT BLANK.

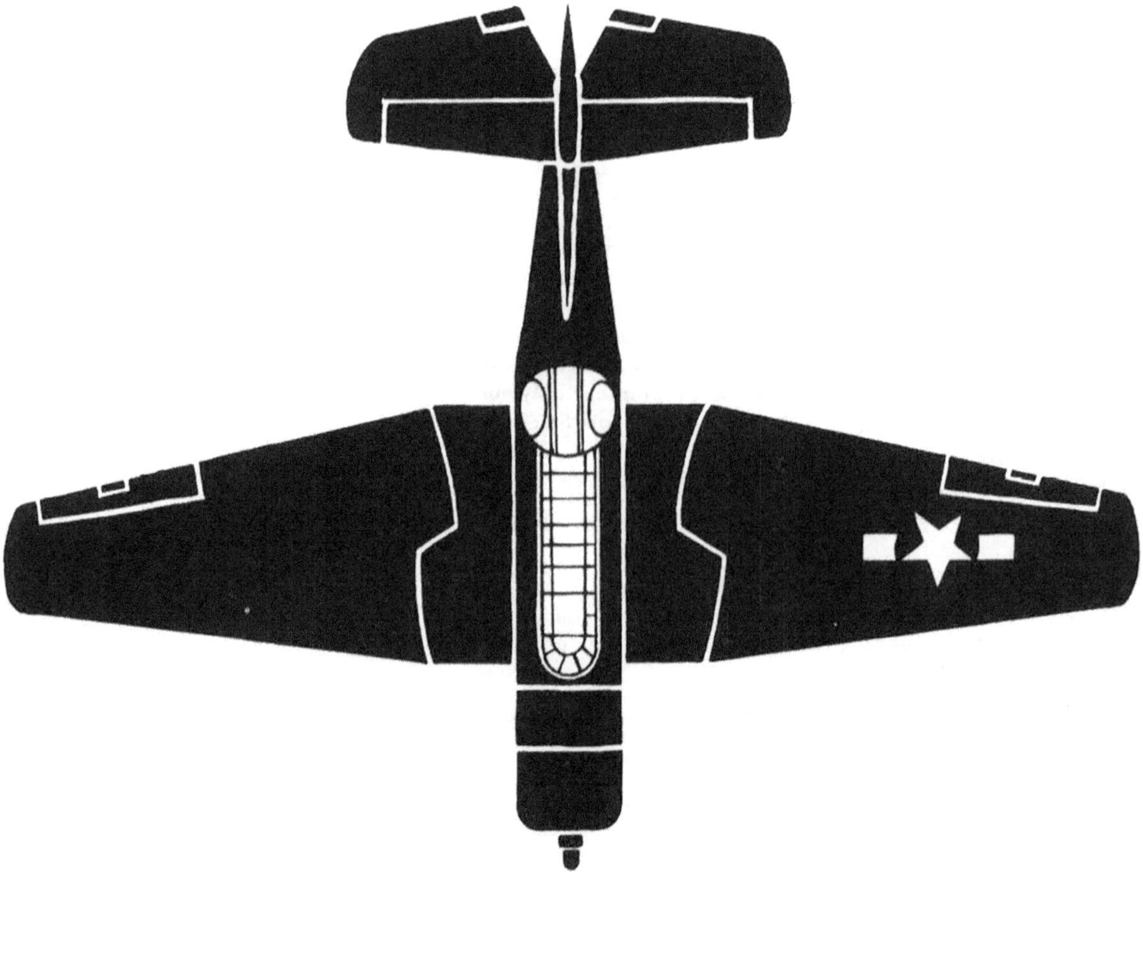

WARNING

The outboard rocket cannot be carried when the Radar Cartridge is secured to the starboard wing panel as the rocket fins would foul on the Radar Cable upon discharge.

6. OPERATION OF COMMUNICATIONS, NAVIGATION, RADAR, AND IFF EQUIPMENT.

a. COMMUNICATIONS EQUIPMENT. — The radio equipment on the TBM-3 airplane consists of the Radio Communication system, the Radio Navigational system, the Radar equipment and IFF equipment.

Communication with other airplanes and ground stations is provided by the three independent radio sets. They are the AN/ART-13 transmitter, ARB and AN/ARC-5 (Yardeny Spot Tuned) Receiver; the AN/ARC-1, VHF Transmitter-Receiver; and the AN/APX-2 IFF equipment. The above system applies to airplane, Serial No. 85602 and subsequent.

The RL-7 interphone system permits two-way intercommunication between pilot and crew. Radio communication from the crew control locations is permitted through the pilot's AN/ARC-5 control unit.

Radio navigational equipment consists of the AN/ARR-2 Receiver and AN/APN-1 Altimeter.

(1) AN/ART-13 TRANSMITTER.—This radio transmitting equipment consists of the following:

A transmitter, dynamotor with power control unit incorporated in its base, pilot's control, fixed antenna and capacitor units.

The AN/ART-13 transmitter, located in the bombardier's compartment, has ten pre-set auto-tune positions for transmission on ten channels which can be changed through the Pilot's control (see Figure 64) or at the transmitter front panel. There is also a manual position which permits tuning, at the transmitter, without disturbing the pre-set channels. Types of emission are modulated Voice, CW (continuous wave) and MCW (modulated continuous wave). Frequency range is from 2000 to 18100 KC.

WARNING

Operation of this equipment involves the use of high voltages. When tuning up the antenna circuit of the transmitter keep personnel clear, as touching the antenna may result in severe burns. Be sure that dynamotor is NOT running before making any adjustment other than tuning up.

(2) ARB RECEIVER.—This receiver is located in the bombardier's compartment and operates through the fixed antenna. Types of its reception are Voice, CW and MCW signals in the frequency range of from 190 KC to 9050 KC, the frequency range being divided into four bands. Operation and selection of stations is remotely controlled by a control unit (see Figure 66) and tuning head (see Figure 65) in the pilot's cockpit, starboard side. Tuning can also be controlled at the receiver front panel.

The pilot's control unit incorporates the following:

(*a*) BAND SELECTOR.—A six position switch by which any of the four bands may be selected.

(*b*) MVC-AVC.—A six position switch with CW and MCW positions using the Manual Volume Control circuit, SHARP and BROAD positions for use with the Automatic Volume Control circuits when MCW signals are being located, and an OFF position.

CAUTION

Certain combinations of the settings of the Band Selector Switch and the MVC-AVC switch can NOT be obtained. This is a normal condition and no attempt should be made to force these switches into any position to which they can not be moved by normal pressure.

(*c*) VOLUME.—Control knob for signal levels in the head phones only, when at MVC positions.

(3) AN/ARR-2 RECEIVER.—This unit is located in the bombardier's compartment under the turret. It receives CW (continuous wave) signals on six bands. A tuning control crank, located on the pilot's AN/ARC-5 control unit, (see Figure 68) is turned to change bands. The ZB antenna rod is used with this receiver.

(4) AN/ARC-5 UNITS.

(*a*) AN/ARC-5 RECEIVER.—This unit is located in the bombardier's compartment under the turret. It has attached to it the C-131/AR Yardeny Spot Tuner unit which provides reception on six preset channels. The control for this unit is shown in Figure 64. It functions with the six preset channels of the AN/ART-13 Transmitter control.

(*b*) AN/ARC-5 CONTROL UNIT, PILOT'S.—This unit (see Figure 68) controls the AN/ARR-2 Receiver, the AN/ARC-1 VHF Transmitter-Receiver, the AN/ARC-5 Receiver, and the Interphone system. It is located on the starboard side of the pilot's cockpit, see Figure 63.

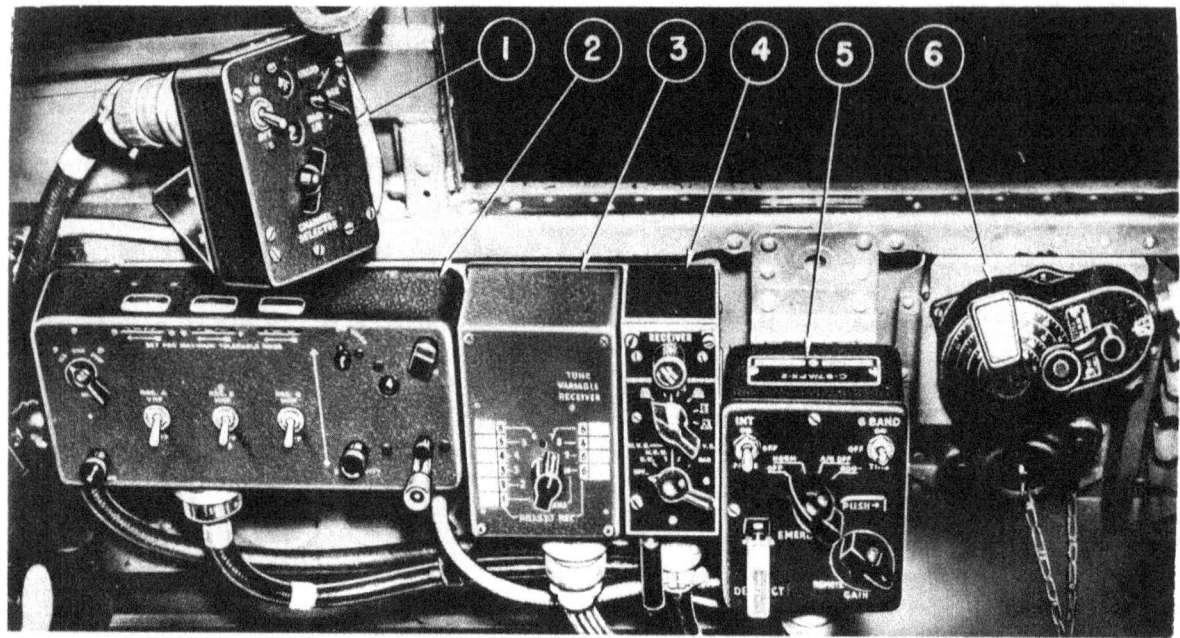

1 AN/ARC-1 Pilot's Control Unit
2 AN/ARC-5 Pilot's Receiver Control Unit
3 AN/ART-13 Transmitter Control Unit and AN/ARC-5 Yardeny Tuned Receiver Control
4 ARB Receiver Control Unit
5 IFF Control Unit
6 ARB Receiver Remote Tuner

Figure 63 — Pilot's Radio Control Units

(c) AN/ARC-5 CONTROL UNITS, OPERATOR'S.—These control boxes (see Figure 69) are used for intercommunication and radio communication through the pilot's control. They are conveniently located for turret gunner and radio man.

(d) AN/ARC-5 JUNCTION BOX.—This unit is used to interconnect the radio equipment. It is located forward of the bombardier's compartment in the passageway to the second cockpit.

(e) POWER FILTER UNIT.—The power filter units are located in the bombardier's compartment.

(f) PILOT'S AN/ARC-5 JACK BOX.—This unit controls the pilot's reception and transmission circuits. It is mounted on the pilot's seat assembly, beneath the right arm rest.

(5) RL-7 INTERPHONE.—An all purpose intercommunication system is available to each crew member through the use of an interphone amplifier and three station control units. The RL-7 Amplifier is mounted on the horizontal bulkhead in the bombardier's compartment on a bracket above the dynamotor for the transmitter.

(6) AN/ARC-1 UNITS.—This unit is used to receive and transmit Voice signals on VHF.

(a) AN/ARC-1 TRANSMITTER-RECEIVER. This unit receives and transmits Voice signals on Very High Frequency, operating on nine main channels and one guard channel. It is mounted on the folding shelf in the second cockpit. The fixed antenna mass on the top of the crash bulkhead is adapted for use as the antenna for this unit.

(b) AN/ARC-1 CONTROL UNIT.—The control for this equipment is mounted on the starboard side of the pilot's cockpit, see Figure 63. It contains the channel selector switch and other control switches as shown in Figure 67.

(7) AN/APX-2 TRANSPONDER.—This IFF equipment is located under the crash bulkhead in the second cockpit. The pilot's control unit C57/APX-2 s mounted on the starboard side of the pilot's cockpit. Bombardier's control box C56/APX-2 is located in the bombardier's compartment. Antennae for this equipment are located on the starboard bomb bay door.

CAUTION

The DESTRUCT switch for the inertia circuit is contained in the pilot's control unit. Throwing this switch to its ON position and jarring the ball in the impact switch off center, sets off a detonator which will destroy the transponder unit internally. No damage will be done to the airplane or personnel. The DESTRUCT switch is connected directly to the batteries and is operative at all times.

(8) AN/APS-4 RADAR.—The AN/APS-4 equipment is a search type radar. The apparatus provides to the pilot and to the radar operator, visual indications of the locations of targets in terms of azimuth (degrees) and range (nautical miles). This equipment consists of a Transmitter-Receiver, Junction Box Control Box, Pilot's Indicator, Pilot's Indicator Amplifier, Operator's Indicator, and Operator's Indicator Amplifier.

(a) RT-5A/APS-4 TRANSMITTER-RECEIVER. This unit is installed just outboard of the R.P. installation on the under surface of the outer starboard wing panel. The unit is secured to a Mk 51 Bomb Rack.

The Transmitter-Receiver unit can be jettisoned from the airplane by employing the following procedure:

1. Close the "Container-Guns-Radar-Wing Bomb Release" switch, located on the pilot's distribution panel.

2. Close the "Armament Master" Switch, located on the pilot's distribution panel.

3. Press and release the "Bomb Release" button on the top aft side of the control stick.

(b) INDICATOR ID-11/APS-4.—An indicator is used at the pilot's position and the radar operator's position in the bombardier's compartment.

An intensity potentiometer is built into the indicator.

(c) INDICATOR AMPLIFIER AN-5A/APS-4. This unit (one for each indicator) is installed adjacent to the indicator scopes.

(d) CONTROL BOX C-12/APS-4.—This unit is located at the operator's position on the starboard side of the bombardier's compartment. It contains the switches that control the operation of the system, a Receiver gain knob, a frequency range selector (FRS) knob, an antenna TILT knob, and an alarm warning light.

(e) JUNCTION BOX J84/APS-4.—This unit is located at the operator's position in the passageway to the second cockpit just forward of the bombardier's.

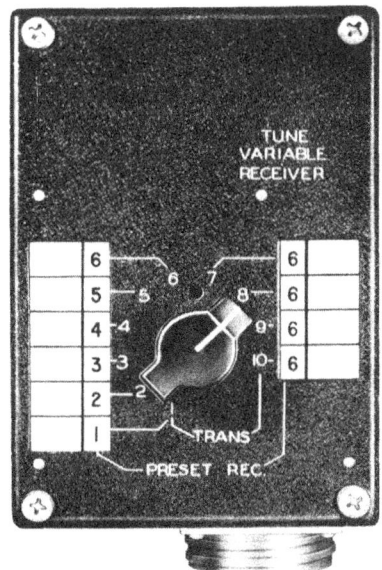

Figure 64 — Pilot's Transmitter Control Unit

Figure 65 — Receiver Tuning Head

Figure 66 — Pilot's Receiver Control Unit

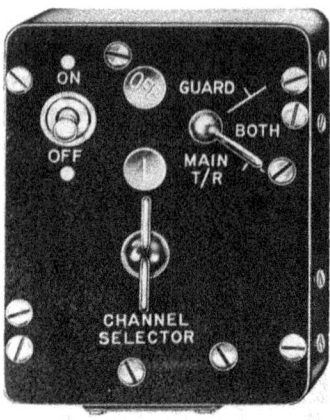

Figure 67 — Pilot's AN/ARC-1 Control Unit

compartment. It is used to provide a means for interconnecting the various units and contains the fuses in the incoming power leads.

(9) AN/APN-1 RADIO ALTIMETER. — The transmitter-receiver unit for this equipment is located on the folding shelf inside of the crash bulkhead. The indicator, ON-OFF switch, limit switch and indicating lights are mounted on the pilot's instrument panel, starboard side. Altimeter antennae assemblies are mounted, one on the under side of each wing outer panel.

b. PILOT'S INSTRUCTIONS.—NORMAL OPERATION OF RADIO NAVIGATION AND COMMUNICATION CONTROLS FROM WARM-UP TO LANDING.

NOTE

These instructions are based on a combat and ferry installation. Since most of the equipment is common to both installations, the instructions that follow apply to both, where the procedure differs, each will be described. These airplanes as delivered to the fleet are provided with the ferry installation, which permits low-frequency range flying in addition to the features provided in the combat installation.

(1) UPON ENTERING COCKPIT, plug the headset into the phone extension cord leading to the Jack Box. Make certain that the microphone and head-set plugs are fully engaged in the Jack Box. If the use of a mask or lip microphone is anticipated, connect either one to the mask microphone cord.

(2) POWER FOR RADIO.—With the battery switch on, engine running, and generator charging, turn on the Radio Master Switch located on the Pilot's Electrical Switch Panel. This supplies power to all radio and interphone equipment in the airplane. While waiting about one minute for the equipment to warm-up, turn off all audio outputs by the following procedure: On the ARC-5 Receiver Control Unit, (Item 3, Fig. 63) turn the "SENSITIVITY" control counterclockwise to minimum. Throw the toggle switches marked "REC A", "REC B", and "REC C" to "OFF". In the Ferry Installation, the "INCREASE OUTPUT" control on the ARB Control Box should be at minimum (full counterclockwise).

(3) INTERPHONE TEST.—On the Receiver Control Unit, set the "ICS-VHF-MHF" microphone switch on "ICS"; press the press-to-talk switch on the microphone and call the radio operator. Release the press-to-talk switch while awaiting a reply. The ICS system should also be checked using the mask or lip microphone if such is provided. In this case, the throttle switch must be pressed in order to talk.

CAUTION

Both pilot and radio operator should take care that neither of their respective "ICS-VHF-MHF" switches is set accidentally on "VHF" or "MHF" to avoid inadvertent radio transmission.

(4) RECEIVER "A" TEST—(VHF AN/ARC-1). For an actual operating test of this equipment, it is necessary that signals be present on the channels on which operation is contemplated. In the absence of signals, the squelch circuit reduces the receiver output to zero so that it is impractical to properly gage receiver performance. The following instructions will illustrate the procedure even though signals are not present.

(*a*) On the Receiver Control Unit, throw the left-hand toggle switch to "REC A". On the VHF Control Unit, make certain that the "ON-OFF" switch is "ON". Throw the "GUARD-BOTH-MAIN T/R" switch to "GUARD". When this is done, "T/R" will appear in the upper window indicating that the equipment is set up for transmission and reception on the

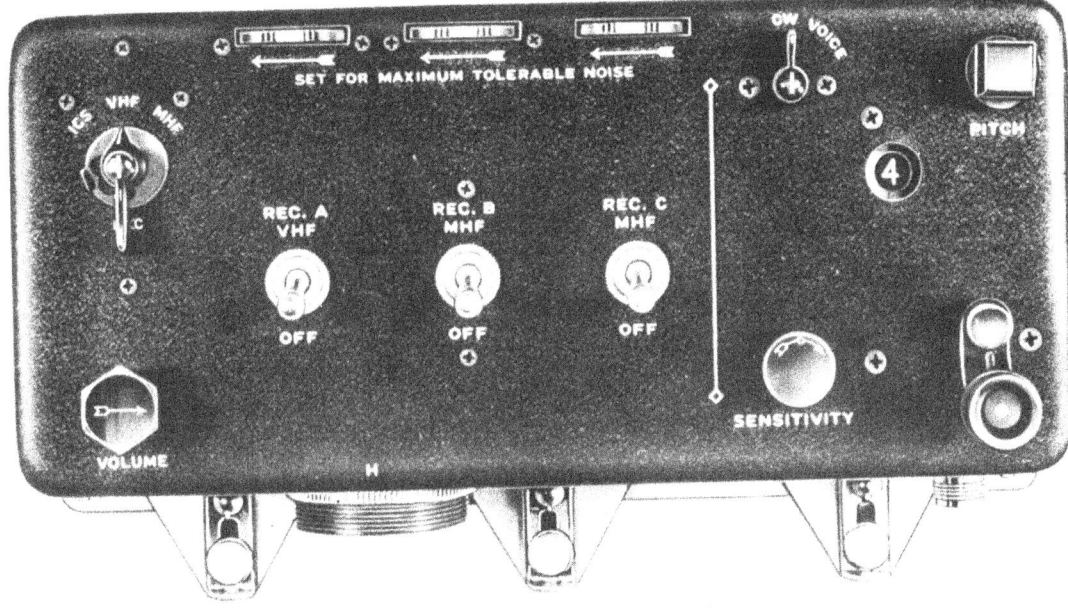

Figure 68 — Pilot's AN/ARC-5 Control Unit

guard channel. "OFF" shows in the lower window, indicating that the main channel is disabled. If a signal is present, advance the "VOLUME" control to obtain the greatest headset volume that can be obtained without aural discomfort. A high setting of this common "VOLUME" control is desirable to keep the output from the other two receivers, especially the AN/ARC-5 receiver, at a satisfactory level.

(*b*) If a signal is not present, advance the "VOLUME" control to maximum (full clockwise). Throw the "GUARD-BOTH-MAIN T/R" switch to "MAIN T/R" and rotate the "CHANNEL SELECTOR" switch until the assigned channel number appears in the lower window. "OFF" will appear in the upper window indicating that the guard channel is disabled. The equipment is now set up for transmission and reception on the main channel indicated.

(*c*) During normal operation, the "GUARD-BOTH-MAIN T/R" switch should be set on "BOTH". When the switch is so set, the guard channel output is combined with the main channel output selected by the "CHANNEL SELECTOR" switch, thus enabling the pilot to monitor the guard and main channels simultaneously. In the event that signals appear simultaneously on both channels causing mutual interference in the headphones, the switch may be thrown

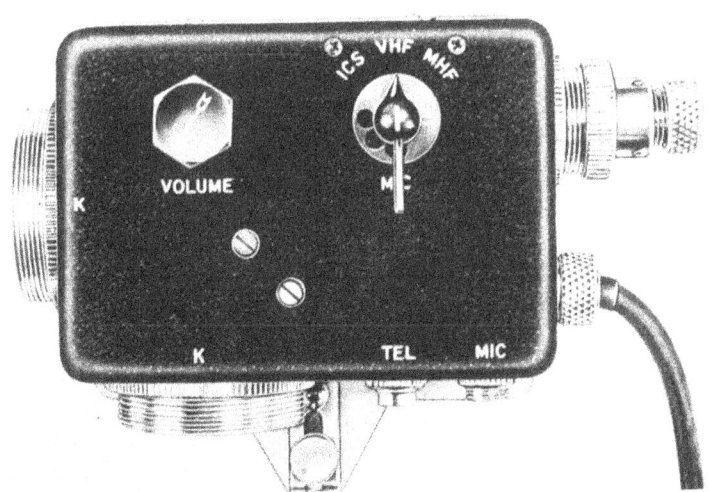

Figure 69 — Operator's AN/ARC-5 Control Unit

to either "GUARD" or "MAIN T/R" depending on which channel the pilot desires to receive free from interference. With the switch in either the "BOTH" or "MAIN T/R" positions, transmission is possible on the main channel selected. When satisfied that the VHF Receiving equipment is functioning satisfactorily, throw the left-hand toggle switch on the Receiver Control Unit to "OFF". Do not disturb the "VOLUME" control setting.

(5) For Combat Installation continue in accordance with procedure (*a*) below; for Ferry Installation continue in accordance with procedure (*b*) below:

(*a*) RECEIVER "B" TEST (ARB)—COMBAT INSTALLATION.—

On the Receiver Control Unit, throw the middle toggle switch to REC B, and adjust the control (just above the toggle switch) marked SET FOR MAX. TOLERABLE NOISE. *If this Control is not set for the maximum noise that can be received with comfort, weak signals may not be heard.* The VOLUME control should be disturbed as little as possible from the setting found satisfactory when the VHF Receiver was tested, consistent with obtaining adequate volume from the ARB Receiver. Throw the REC B toggle switch to OFF, thus completing the adjustments and test of the ARB Receiver. Next set up receiver C (see paragraph (6) below).

(*b*) ARB RECEIVER TEST—FERRY INSTALLATION.

1. Certain combinations of the setting of the HOMING-COMMUN and MVC-AVC switches on the ARB Control Box cannot be obtained. This is a normal condition and no attempt should be made to force these switches into any positions to which they cannot be moved by normal pressure. The two positions under HOMING on the HOMING-COMMUN switch are not used in this installation; no antenna is provided for these positions. Detailed instructions follow:

a. MCW AND VOICE RECEPTION.—Set the HOMING—COMMUN switch on one of the four bands under COMMUN on which reception is desired. If the band selected is either 195-500 kc or 560-1600 kc, set the MVC—AVC switch on MCW and tune in the signal by means of the ARB tuning head. Perform this final tuning with the INCREASE OUTPUT control reduced to a low but comfortable volume level. If the band selected is either 1.6-4.5 mc or 4.9-9.05 mc, set the MVC—AVC switch in the BROAD position when searching for the signal. When the signal has been located, shift the MVC—AVC switch to MCW and perform the final tuning as described above. For voice reception, shift the MVC—AVC switch to SHARP. Shifting from MVC to AVC operation, or vice versa, may require adjustment of the INCREASE OUTPUT control to maintain satisfactory volume level in the headphones.

b. RANGE RECEPTION.—The procedure is similar to that given above except that MVC—AVC switch must be set on MCW while receiving range signals. *Under no circumstances should range reception be attempted with the MVC—AVC switch on any AVC position.* The INCREASE OUTPUT control should be set to the minimum value required for reception.

c. CW RECEPTION.—Set the HOMING—COMMUN switch to the desired band under COMMUN. Set the MVC—AVC switch on CW. Advance the INCREASE OUTPUT control until normal background noise is heard. Tune in the desired signal and readjust the INCREASE OUTPUT control for a comfortable volume level.

2. When satisfied that the receiver is performing satisfactorily, rotate the INCREASE OUTPUT control to minimum (full counterclockwise), thus completing adjustments and test of the ARB receiver.

(6) RECEIVER "C" TEST. (MHF Unit of AN/ARC-5)—On the Receiver Control Unit, throw the right-hand toggle switch to REC C. Adjust the control (just above the toggle switch) marked SET FOR MAX. TOLERABLE NOISE. *If this control is not set for the maximum noise that can be received with comfort, weak signals may not be heard.* The VOLUME control should be disturbed as little as possible from the setting found satisfactory when the VHF Receiver was tested, consistent with obtaining adequate volume from the AN/ARC-5 Receiver. On the MHF transmitter-receiver control unit (Item 3, Fig. 63) set the channel selector on the desired channel from 1 to 6. Throw the REC C toggle switch to OFF at the conclusion of the test.

(7) For Combat Installation continue in accordance with procedure (*a*) below; for Ferry Installation continue in accordance with procedure (*b*) below:

(*a*) NAVIGATION RECEIVER TEST (AN/ARR-2)—COMBAT INSTALLATION.—

On the Receiver Control Unit, operate the crank in the right-hand section of the unit to bring the assigned channel number in the indicator window. Set the CW-VOICE switch to CW. Set the SENSITIVITY knob (located to the left of the tuning crank) to obtain a usable weak signal, or if the desired signal cannot be heard, to a fairly strong background hiss. Do not disturb the VOLUME control setting. If a signal is present, adjust the PITCH control to produce a pleasing audible tone. Readjust the SENSITIVITY control to keep the signal rather weak. *If the signal is too strong, a clear-cut course indication cannot be obtained.* The secret in accurate interpretation of navigation signals lies in the use of the* least*

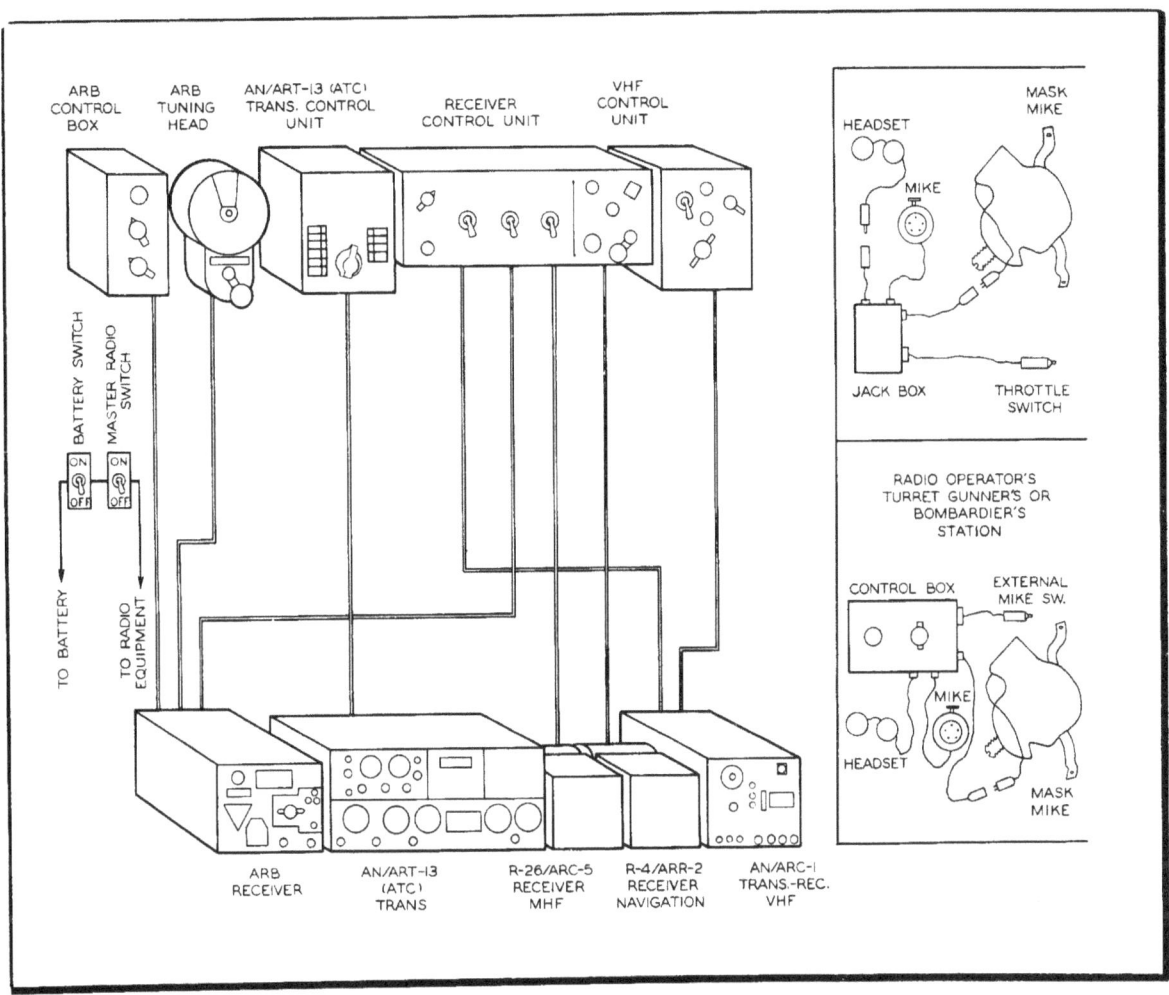

Figure 70 — Communications Equipment, Schematic

setting of the SENSITIVITY control. Keep this control adjusted to receive only one character predominantly. The lower the signal level, the better the operation. When satisfied that the Navigation Receiver is operating properly, proceed as described in paragraph (8) below. Do not disturb the above adjustments.

(b) FERRY INSTALLATION.—On the Receiver Control Unit, make certain that the SENSITIVITY control is off (full counterclockwise), thus omitting the Navigation Receiver from the line-up.

(8) For Combat Installation continue in accordance with procedure (*a*) below; for Ferry Installation continue in accordance with procedure (*b*) below:

(a) SIMULTANEOUS OPERATION.—COMBAT INSTALLATION.—

On the Receiver Control Unit, throw the three toggle switches to REC A, REC B, and REC C respectively.

(b) SIMULTANEOUS OPERATION.—FERRY INSTALLATION.—

On the Receiver Control Unit, throw the left-hand and right-hand toggle switches to REC A and REC C respectively. REC B toggle switch is inoperative for ferry installation. On the ARB Receiver Control Box, turn up the INCREASE OUTPUT control for normal operation (see sub-paragraph (5) (*b*) above).

(9) VHF TRANSMISSION (AN/ARC-1).

WARNING

The instructions for operating transmitters are subject to local limitations regarding *radio silence.*

Voice transmission only is provided by the VHF equipment. The receiving equipment should be in operation as described above. On the VHF Control Unit, select the channel on which transmission is desired in accordance with the instructions in paragraph (4) above. On the Receiver Control Unit, place the ICS-VHF-MHF microphone switch on VHF. Press the press-to-talk switch on the hand-held microphone and proceed with the transmission. If a mask or a lip microphone is used in place of the hand-held microphone, press the throttle switch.

(10) MHF TRANSMISSION. (AN/ART-13, ATC). — The following instructions assume that the LOCAL-REMOTE switch located on the transmitter front panel has been placed in the REMOTE position. On the AN/ART-13 Transmitter Control Unit, select the desired channel by means of the CHANNEL switch. After about 25 seconds the transmitter is set up on the channel selected. While waiting for the switching operation to be completed, be sure the emission selector switch, just above the CHANNEL selector switch is set on VOICE. On the Receiver Control Unit place the ICS-VHF-MHF switch on MHF and proceed with transmission. Press the press-to-talk switch on the hand-held microphone and talk. Release the switch to listen. If a lip or a mask microphone is used, press the throttle switch to talk. Side tone may be heard by throwing REC "C" toggle switch on the Receiver Control Box to REC "C". The first 6 channels of the AN/ART-13 are controlled concurrently with the AN/ARC-5 Yardeny Tuned Receiver. On selecting channels 7 to 10 on the transmitter-receiver control box (Item 3, Figure 63), the operator may receive channel 6 only of the AN/ARC-5 receiver, or he may listen to the variably tuned ARB receiver by throwing REC "B" toggle switch to REC "B" on the Receiver Control Unit. It should be noted that the ARB receiver is not in any way controlled by the MHF Transmitter-Receiver Control Box (Item 3, Figure 63).

(11) PILOT'S CHECK-OFF LIST.

(a) BEFORE TAKE-OFF:

1. Plug in headset and mask or lip microphone if used.

2. Turn ON Master Radio Switch.

3. Test ICS.

4. Test REC A (VHF).

5. Test ARB Receiver (MHF).

6. Test REC C (MHF.)

7. Test Navigation Receiver (if combat installation).

8. Set up for simultaneous operation.

CAUTION
VHF or MHF test transmission in combat areas subject to *Radio Silence* regulations.

9. Make VHF test transmission.

10. Make AN/ART-13 test transmission (MHF).

(b) AFTER LANDING:

Turn OFF Radio Master Switch.

c. OPERATION OF AN/APS-4 RADAR, AN/ARR-2 (IFF), AND AN/APN-1 ALTIMETER EQUIPMENT. (OPERATOR CONTROLLED).

(1) AN/APS-4 RADAR EQUIPMENT.—Operators of the AN/APS-4 Radar Equipment must be thoroughly familiar with the equipment's controls on the Control Box, the Indicator-Amplifier and the Indicator. A thorough review of the Equipment Operation Instruction Manual should be made at frequent intervals.

(a) SETTING CONTROLS FOR NON-OPERATIVE CONDITIONS.—Check the positions of the following switches on the control box to insure that the equipment is in an inoperative condition:

1. Test Switch—OFF.

2. Warning—OFF.

3. Beacon Search—SEARCH or BEACON.

4. Intercept-Search—SEARCH.

5. Range—20.

6. Tilt—0.

7. Receiver Gain—Full Counterclockwise.

8. Off-Warm-Up-Run—OFF.

9. Intensity Knob — Full Counterclockwise (both indicators).

(b) TURNING THE EQUIPMENT ON.— Throw the OFF-WARM-UP-RUN switch to the WARM-UP position. After waiting for at least one minute (two to three minutes in extreme cold), throw the switch to the RUN position.

(c) IF SURFACE TARGETS ARE SOUGHT:

1. Turn the OFF-WARM-UP-RUN switch to WARM-UP.

2. Place the TEST switch on OFF.

3. Place the BEACON-SEARCH switch on SEARCH.

4. Place the INTERCEPT-SEARCH switch on SEARCH.

5. Place the RANGE switch on 20.

6. Place the TILT control on —10.

7. Turn the RECEIVER GAIN control about 45 degrees to the left of its vertical position.

8. One minute after turning the OFF-WARM-UP-RUN switch to WARM-UP, (two or three minutes in extreme cold), turn it to RUN.

9. Turn the intensity control on the indicator to illuminate moderately the indicator screen.

(d) IF AIR TARGETS ARE SOUGHT:

1. Turn the OFF-WARM-UP-RUN switch to WARM-UP.

2. Place the TEST switch on OFF.

3. Place the BEACON-SEARCH switch on SEARCH.

4. Place the INTERCEPT-SEARCH switch on INTERCEPT.

5. Place the RANGE switch on 4.

6. Place the TILT control on 0.

7. Place the RECEIVER GAIN control about 45 degrees to the left of its vertical position.

8. One minute after turning the OFF-WARM-UP-RUN switch to WARM-UP (two or three minutes in extreme cold), turn it to RUN.

9. Turn the intensity control on the indicator to illuminate moderately the indicator screen.

10. Operate the TILT control for optimum results.

(e) IF BEACON HOMING IS DESIRED:

1. Turn the OFF-WARM-UP-RUN switch to WARM-UP.

2. Place the TEST switch on OFF.

3. Place the BEACON-SEARCH switch on BEACON.

4. Place the INTERCEPT-SEARCH switch on SEARCH.

5. Place the RANGE switch on 50.

6. Place the TILT control on 0.

7. Place the RECEIVER GAIN control 45 degrees to the left of vertical.

8. One minute after turning the OFF-WARM-UP-RUN switch to WARM-UP (two or three minutes in extreme cold), turn it to RUN.

9. Turn the intensity control on the indicator to illuminate moderately the indicator screen.

(f) TURNING OFF THE EQUIPMENT:

1. Turn the OFF-WARM-UP-RUN switch to OFF.

2. Turn the intensity controls on both indicators to the extreme counterclockwise positions.

3. Turn the RECEIVER GAIN control to its extreme counterclockwise position.

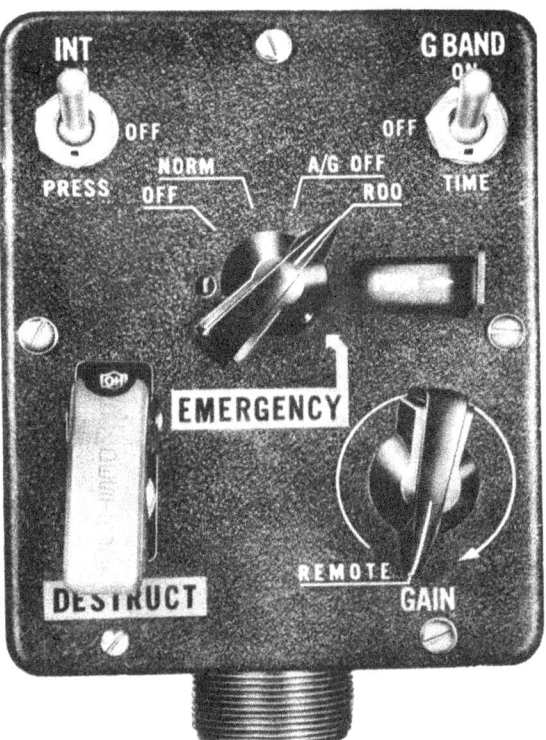

Figure 72 — IFF Pilot's Control

(g) ABNORMAL OPERATION.—Throw the OFF-WARM-UP-RUN switch to the OFF position immediately if any abnormal operation is observed. Report any abnormal operation to the maintenance personnel as soon as possible.

(2) AN/APX-2 IFF EQUIPMENT.—Operators must be thoroughly familiar with the equipment controls. Hence for a complete and comprehensive description of all controls including present maintenance adjustments, the operator should be acquainted with Equipment Operating Manual. The following is an abbreviated operating procedure:

(a) Before actual operation is begun take the following precautions:

1. Check that a complete destructor-firing for the test has been performed in accordance with instructions of Equipment Operating Manuals.

2. On the pilot's control unit check that the guard latch marked PUSH effectively prevents the accidental rotation of the Master Control Switch to its EMERGENCY position and that the red guard cover is closed down over the DESTRUCT switch.

(b) TO START THE EQUIPMENT.—To start the equipment turn the Master Control switch S403 clockwise to any position beyond the OFF position. Normally S403 is rotated to the NORM position.

Further rotation clockwise is done only for designated tactical purposes. The ROO position is used only after certain readjustment has been made inside the Receiver-Transmitter unit by the maintenance crew. The EMERGENCY position is never used except when the aircraft, during flight, is in extreme distress. The pilot will be governed by existing regulations dealing with the Emergency Operation.

(c) TO CHANGE SELECTOR SWITCH POSITIONS.—On the pilot's control unit rotate the selector switch S302 to the position designated by the commanding officer. Unless otherwise designated selector switch is set and left in position one.

(d) FOR INT OPERATION.—On the pilot's control unit throw the INT switch S401 to the ON position; or on the operator's control unit hold the INT switch S301 momentarily on the PRESS position.

(e) FOR G-BAND OPERATION.—On the pilot's control unit throw the G-Band switch to the ON position or flip it to the TIME position, in conformity with tactical considerations. This switch is normally left in the OFF position.

(f) FOR ROO OPERATION.—On the pilot's control unit rotate the Master Switch, S403 to the ROO position (only by specific direction of the commanding officer and only if a specified ROO adjustment has been made inside the Receiver-Transmitter unit by the maintenance crew).

(g) FOR DISTRESS OPERATION.—On the pilot's control unit push the guard latch, marked PUSH, to the right tilting it up and rotate the Master Control switch to the EMERGENCY position (extreme clockwise).

(h) TO DESTROY THE RECEIVER-TRANSMITTER UNIT.—Warn operating personnel to stay clear of the receiver-transmitter unit. On the pilot's control unit raise the red guard cover and throw the DESTRUCT switch to the ON position.

(i) FURTHER OPERATING PROCEDURES.—Information on further operating procedures must be obtained from the commanding officer and the Equipment Maintenance Manual.

(j) TO STOP THE EQUIPMENT.—On the pilot's control unit rotate the Master Control Switch to extreme counterclockwise position marked OFF.

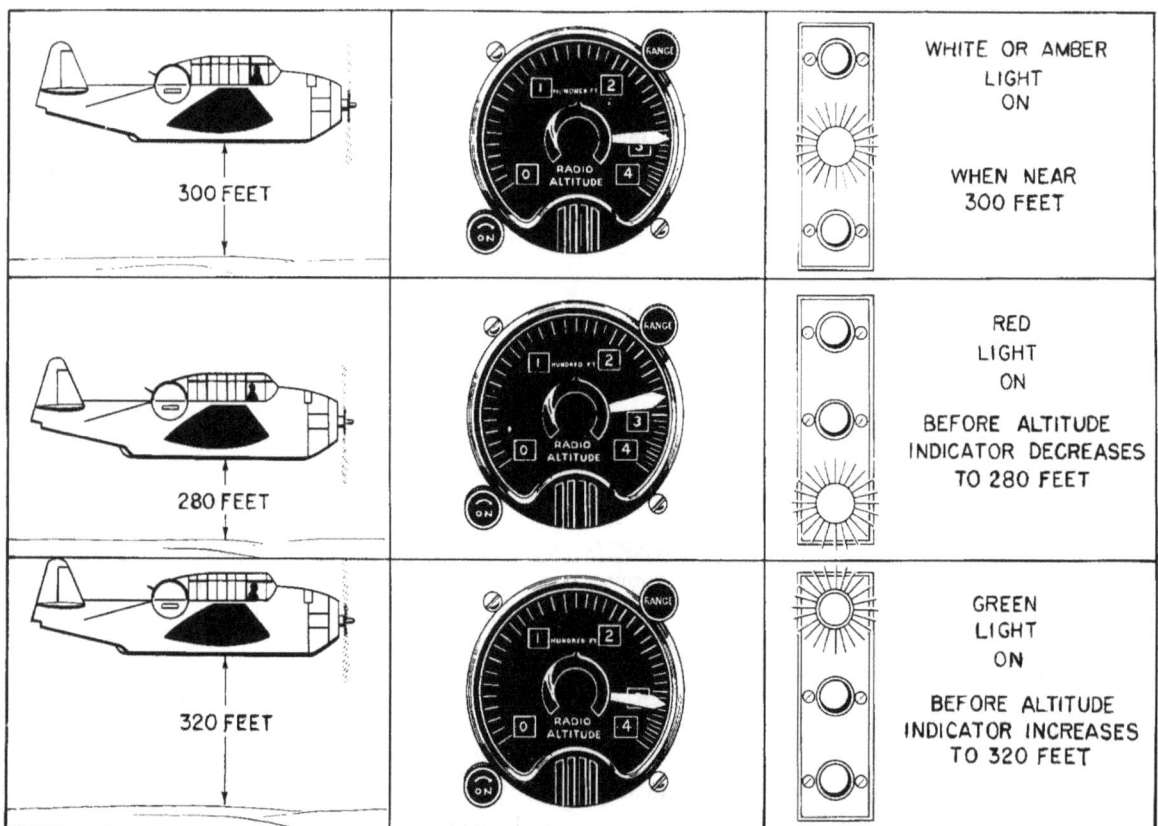

Figure 73 — AN/APN-1 Altimeter Operation

(3) AN/APN-1, RADIO ALTIMETER RADIO.

(*a*) The ON-OFF switch is located on the instrument panel between the Altitude Limit Switch and the Altitude Indicator.

(*b*) The ALTITUDE LIMIT SWITCH is used to set a determined altitude at which flight is desired between the range of 50 to 300 feet and 500 to 3000 feet. Indicator lights on the instrument panel indicate the altitude of the airplane as compared to the set altitude:

    Amber—Flight is at SET altitude.
    Green—Flight is ABOVE set altitude.
    Red—Flight is BELOW set altitude.

(*c*) The ALTITUDE INDICATOR incorporates two ranges:

    Low Range—0 to 400 feet.
    High Range—400 to 4000 feet.

(*d*) STARTING THE EQUIPMENT. — To place the altimeter equipment in operation, proceed as follows:

1. RANGE SWITCH.—Set the range switch for the required range. When on the ground, or in flight at an altitude below 400 feet, always use the low range (0 to 400 feet). When in flight at an altitude above 400 feet, use the high range (400 to 4000 feet).

WARNING

The High Range is not calibrated for and must not be used at altitudes below 400 feet. *Under conditions of poor visibility, always use the Low Range when flying at altitudes below 600 feet.*

Figure 74 — Altimeter Controls and Indicator

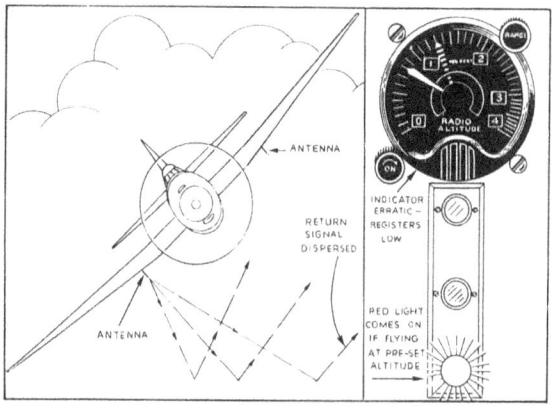

Figure 75 — Erratic Readings in a Steep Bank

2. ALTITUDE LIMIT SWITCH.—Set the Altitude Limit Switch for the desired pre-set altitude. One of the eleven different altitudes may be pre-selected by the switch.

3. POWER.—Turn the power switch clockwise to the "ON" position. A "green" signal will appear immediately on the altitude limit indicator and will be sustained during the warm-up period. After allowing an interval of approximately one minute for the tubes to heat, the pointer of the Altitude Indicator will have moved from its sub-zero stop position to some other position, indicating that the equipment is operating. The altitude limit indicator signals will then function.

Note

When the aircraft is on the ground, the Altitude Indicator pointer may not indicate zero altitude exactly. *Never attempt to adjust the equipment to obtain a zero reading for this condition.*

(*e*) CHANGE OF PRE-SET ALTITUDE.—The setting of the Altitude Limit Switch may be changed at any time to a new pre-set altitude as desired.

(*f*) STOPPING THE EQUIPMENT.—To stop the operation of the altimeter, turn the power switch counterclockwise to the off position.

7. AUTOMATIC PILOT.

a. GENERAL.—This airplane is equipped with a Model G1 automatic pilot, which is designed to provide control of rudder, ailerons and elevators, maintaining directional, lateral and longitudinal stability as set by the human pilot, thereby relieving him of the physical duty of flying.

The automatic pilot gives an instrument indication of all normal movements of the airplane for both manual and automatic flight.

It is operated by hydraulic pressure supplied by the engine-driven pump. Hydraulic pressure of 150 pounds per square inch is required for satisfactory operation.

The ON-OFF-BLEED valve is located on the shelf to the left of the pilot. The BLEED position of the valve maintains the system ready for operation. (This is especially important in cold weather operations) and free from trapped air by constantly circulating the hydraulic fluid through the system.

The controls are located on the upper part of the pilot's instrument panel. (See Fig. 77).

b. OPERATION OF AUTOMATIC PILOT.

(1) BEFORE TAKE-OFF.

(*a*) Check hydraulic pressure on pressure gage at left of pilot; it should be approximately 150 pounds per square inch with valve in ON position. No pressure is indicated when valve is in BLEED or OFF position.

(*b*) Turn automatic pilot switch to INST position and wait 3 minutes to allow the gyros to come up to speed.

(*c*) Pull out the caging knob of the bank-and-climb gyro, turn it counterclockwise as far as it will go, and push it in. It will take several minutes for the horizon bar to complete its movement to indicate the tilt of the airplane in the three point attitude.

(*d*) Turn the course-setting knob of the directional gyro until the dial heading under the lubber line agrees with the magnetic compass. Then pull the knob straight out to uncage the gyro.

(*e*) Set the manual controls in their neutral position. Turn the automatic pilot switch to the SYNC position and wait one minute. Then synchronize the synchronizing indicators. Turn hydraulic selector valve ON.

1. Apply light pressure to the manual controls. The controls should appear locked. If an elastic action is felt in the controls, it is an indication that air is present in the hydraulic servo.

2. To remove air, turn the valve to the BLEED position. Turn all three trim knobs so that synchronizing indicators are not centered. Turn the control switch to AUTO. Move pedals and stick from hardover to hardover holding at each extreme for 25 to 30 seconds. This allows time for air to be carried to the sump. Re-synchronize and turn oil valve ON. Check to see if all air has been removed.

(*f*) Check the overpower valves in the hydraulic servo. A rapidly applied heavy pressure on the manual control should permit overpowering of the automatic pilot.

(*g*) Check the direction of controls by turning the instrument trim knobs in both directions and observing the control surfaces.

(*h*) Turn hydraulic selector valve OFF. Turn the automatic pilot selector switch to INST.

(2) FOR TAKE-OFF.

WARNING

Hydraulic pressure MUST be OFF and gyros UNCAGED at least 3 minutes before taking off.

(3) AFTER TAKE-OFF.

(*a*) MANUAL FLYING.

1. The bank-and-climb gyro provides an artificial horizon with a zero pitch adjustment to enable adjustments that may vary due to altitude, loading and power.

2. The directional gyro control unit provides a deadbeat directional reference.

Note

The directional gyro heading should be checked at 15 or 20 minute intervals with the magnetic compass to see whether the course has changed appreciably.

(*b*) AUTOMATIC FLYING.

1. Make sure that the hydraulic pressure is OFF.

2. Put the gyros into operation as flight instruments.

3. Trim airplane "hands off" with the trim tabs.

4. Set the 3 sensitivity controls slightly counterclockwise from the center of their travel.

WARNING

Never touch the sensitivity controls unless an adjustment is made necessary by a flutter of the control surfaces or by the airplane's hunting. Do not adjust them near the earth as a sudden change of attitude may result. Turn them slowly and cautiously.

5. Turn instrument selector switch to SYNC.

6. Wait one minute. Turn the rudder trim-control knob continuously in one direction until the synchronizing-indicator pointer moves across the scale in the direction that the top of the knob is turned. Then turn it back just enough to make the pointer move back across or just stay on the scale.

7. Turn the aileron and elevator trim-control knobs until the pointers just cross or stay on the scales.

Note

It is impossible to fly an airplane manually with such accuracy that the autopilot will not give a full electrical signal one way or the other. For this reason it is difficult to place the synchronizing-indicator pointer on zero.

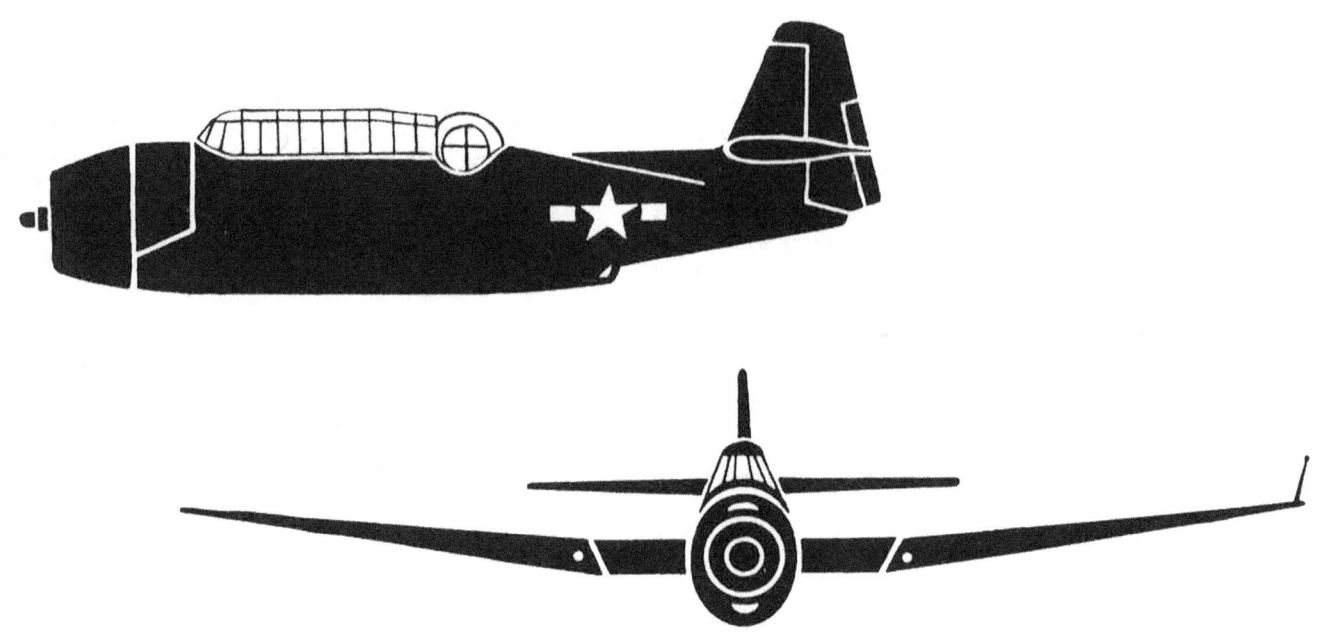

THIS PAGE INTENTIONALLY LEFT BLANK.

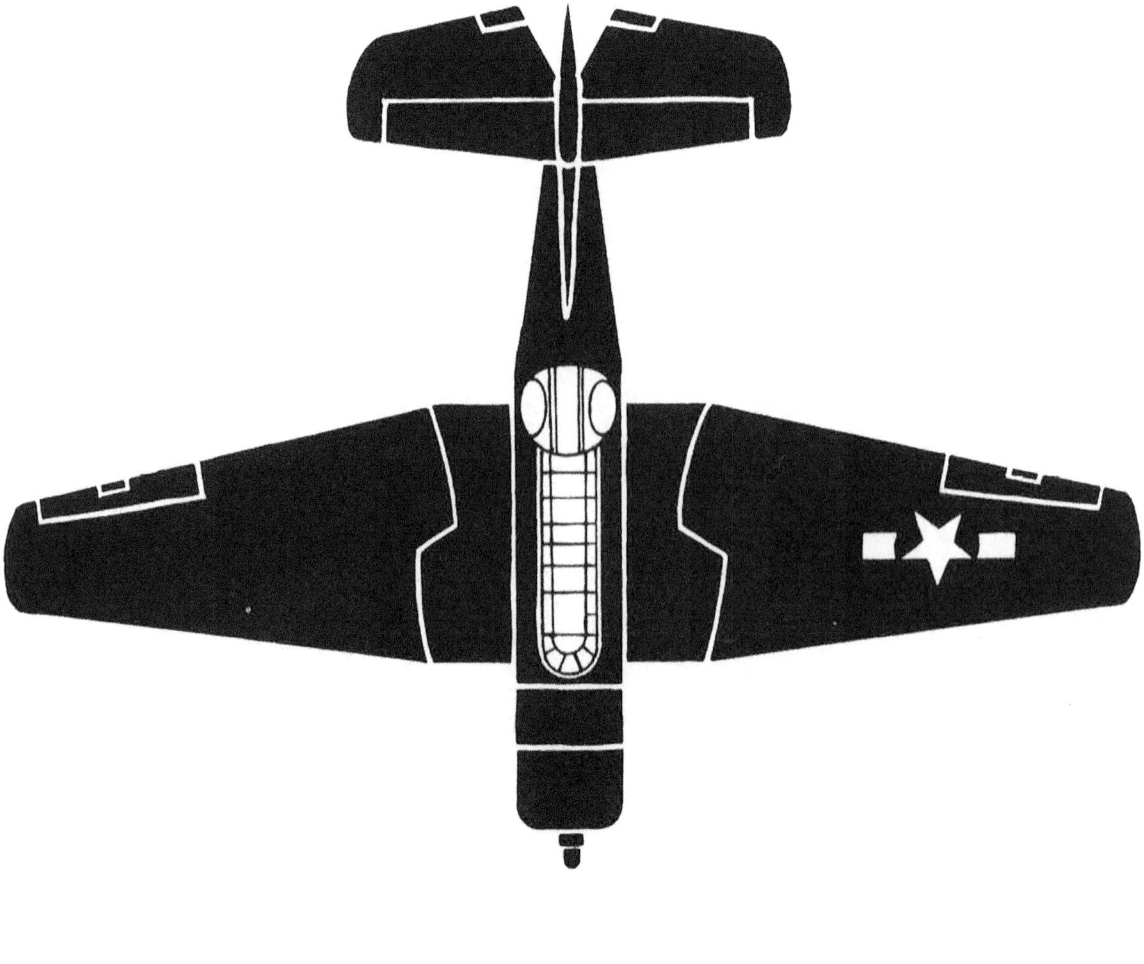

However exact synchronizing is unnecessary. If a small movement of the trim-control knobs throws the indicator pointers from one side to the other the attitude of the airplane will change only a fraction of a degree when the selector valve is turned ON.

8. Turn the hydraulic selector valve ON. This gives the airplane "Soft-pilot" automatic pilot.

9. Turn the instrument selector switch to AUTO. When the automatic pilot is engaged there may be an oscillation of one or more of the controls. Slowly turn the sensitivity knob, corresponding to the oscillating control, counterclockwise until oscillation ceases. Turning the sensitivity back too far may cause hunting of the airplane. The best adjustment of the sensitivity knob is approximately at the 12 o'clock position.

10. Adjust the sensitivity knobs for the most comfort in the prevailing weather conditions. The airplane should be stable about any of its three axes without oscillation or hunting in its controls.

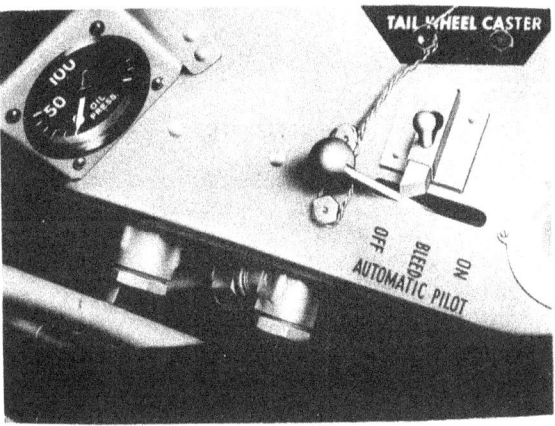

Figure 76 — Automatic Pilot Control and Hydraulic Gage

(4) OPERATION LIMITS.

(*a*) The automatic pilot can be used for maneuvering in dive, climb or bank, not exceeding 60 degrees.

Note

After returning to level flight from a maneuver which involves a bank greater than 45° the horizontal bar may be off from the true position. This error will always indicate left wing down regardless of direction of previous turn. The gyro will return to the true position slowly.

(*b*) The instrument stops allow freedom of motion through the use of manual controls in bank-and-climb gyro up to 90 degrees in bank and up to 60 degrees in climb or dive and in the directional gyro up to 60 degrees in bank, climb or dive.

CAUTION

For maneuvers beyond the set limits, the gyro units must be caged to prevent upsetting the gyros.

(*c*) The automatic pilot does not compensate for loss of altitude when the ship is flying in normal position.

(*d*) If a disturbance should cause the airplane to change attitude so much that a gyro hits a stop and precession sets in, take these steps at once:

1. Quickly turn the hydraulic selector valve OFF and right the airplane manually.

2. Cage both gyros to restore their equilibrium.

3. If gyros are to be taken out of service turn the control switch OFF.

4. If the gyros are to be used as flight instruments, turn the control switch to INST. Then set and uncage the gyros.

5. If the autopilot is to be put back in control, switch to SYNC and proceed as previously instructed.

(5) DIRECTIONAL CONTROL.

(*a*) Directional control is taken from the directional gyro unit which is set to agree with the magnetic compass. It is set by turning the caging and course setting knob when the knob is at its innermost position.

Note

The caging and course setting knob has a dual function. (1) Course setting PUSH in and turn to desired direction, (2) uncaging gyro PULL directly out without rotating the knob.

(*b*) The average drift of the directional gyro is 3 degrees in 15 minutes, due to the rotation of the earth. The instrument must be reset periodically to the magnetic heading by turning the course setting knob. Small angular deflections can be compensated with rudder trim control.

(6) LONGITUDINAL CONTROL.—Longitudinal control with the automatic pilot is taken from the bank-and-climb gyro. The airplane can be maintained in level flight or in climbing or diving by adjusting the instrument trim control.

(7) LATERAL CONTROL.—Lateral control in the automatic pilot is also taken from the bank-and-climb gyro. The airplane can be maintained in level flight laterally or in a right-or left-banking attitude.

(8) TURNS.

(*a*) Flat turns of a few degrees are made by adjusting only the rudder trim control. The airplane will turn until the new course is reached and will then resume straight flight. For turns of greater magnitude, bank must be introduced by the AILERON trim knob and as the plane assumes its new course, it should be levelled by adjusting the AILERON trim control. It is

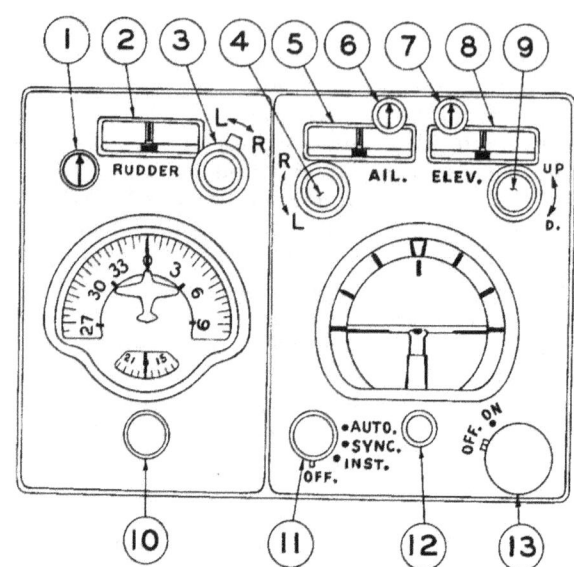

1. Rudder Sensitivity Control.
2. Rudder Synchronizing Indicator
3. Rudder Trim Control Knob
4. Aileron Trim Control Knob
5. Aileron Synchronizing Indicator
6. Aileron Sensitivity Control
7. Elevator Sensitivity Control
8. Elevator Synchronizing Indicator
9. Elevator Trim Control Knob
10. Push to Cage Directional Gyro
11. Control Switch
12. Load Indicator
13. Rotate Clockwise to Cage Bank-and-Climb Gyro

Figure 77 — Automatic Pilot Control

desirable to introduce some elevator in making a banked turn to compensate for loss of altitude.

(b) Continuous turns are made by caging the directional gyro and turning the RUDDER TRIM control knob until the desired rate of turn is reached. Leave the knob in this position. Proper bank for the turn must be introduced by the AILERON trim knob. It is desirable to introduce some elevator in making a banked turn to compensate for loss of altitude. When turn is complete, uncage directional gyro and level the plane by the AILERON trim.

(c) SPIRALS.—A continuous turn is made into a spiral by introducing the desired climb or glide, using the ELEVATOR trim knob.

(9) DISENGAGING THE AUTOMATIC PILOT.

(a) Turn hydraulic selector valve OFF.

(b) Turn the automatic pilot instrument selector switch to INST in order to use the gyros as flight instruments.

c. CONDENSED OPERATING INSTRUCTIONS

(1) AS FLIGHT INSTRUMENTS.

(a) Turn control switch to INST. Wait three minutes.

(b) Set directional gyro by compass.

(c) Uncage gyros.

(2) AS AUTOPILOT.

(a) Trim airplane to fly hands off.

(b) Start gyros as flight instruments.

(c) Turn control switch to SYNC and wait one minute.

(d) Synchronize—Turn trim control knobs until all indicator pointers are as near center as possible or where slightest motion makes them cross from side to side.

WARNING

Turn rudder trim knob until pointer moves in SAME direction as top of knob.

(e) Turn oil valve slowly ON.

(f) Turn control switch to AUTO.

(3) CONTROL IN FLIGHT.

(a) Use the three trim control knobs to change attitude.

(b) Shut the autopilot OFF before resetting the directional gyro control unit to compass heading.

(4) SHUTTING OFF.

(a) Turn oil valve OFF.

(b) TO RETURN TO USE AS FLIGHT INSTRUMENTS.
   Turn control switch to INST.
   TO SHUT OFF COMPLETELY: Cage gyros and turn control switch OFF.

(5) GYRO STOP LIMITS.
   60° dive or climb.
   60° bank for directional.
   90° bank for bank-and-climb.

(6) SENSITIVITY.

(a) DO NOT turn the sensitivity control knobs unless necessary and NEVER turn full counterclockwise during flight.

(b) Turn clockwise to stop hunting of airplane.

(c) Turn counterclockwise to stop flutter of controls.

8. BOMBING EQUIPMENT.

a. GENERAL.—The bomb bay occupies the lower part of the fuselage from the engine compartment to the bombardier's compartment. The bomb bay doors are hydraulically operated and release of the bombs is controlled electrically by the bombardier or pilot and manually by the pilot only. TBM-3 airplanes Navy Serial Nos. 22857 to 23656, 68062 to 69184 inclusive are designed so that Mark 4 bomb shackles must be used. TBM-3 airplanes Navy Serial 69185 and subsequent are designed so that Mark 8 bomb shackles must be used. Features of both installations will be discussed and illustrated in the following text so that the operation of airplanes employing either type shackle installation, can be accomplished.

Provisions are made for the installation of the following bomb loads in the bomb bay with either shackle installation:

(1) 12—100 lb. Class Bombs.
(2) 4—500 lb. Class Bombs.
(3) 1—1000 lb. G.P. Bomb.
(4) 2—1000 lb. A.P. Bombs.
(5) 1—1600 lb. A.P. Bomb.
(6) 1—2000 lb. G.P. Bomb.
(7) 1—Torpedo Mark 13 Mod. 2.
(8) 2—1000 lb. G.P. Bombs in Tandem.

Note

Those controls which are not common to both types of bomb shackle installations will be so designated.

b. BOMBING CONTROLS.

(1) PILOT'S CONTROLS.

(*a*) BOMB BAY DOOR CONTROL HANDLE. The bomb bay door control handle is located below the main instrument panel just above the left rudder pedal. The bomb bay doors are usually opened by the pilot, but may be opened by the bombardier. A red jewel warning light, located on the right side of the pilot's instrument panel, illuminates when the bomb bay doors are opened.

(*b*) ELECTRICAL SWITCHES.—The distribution panel on the starboard side of the pilot's cockpit contains the armament master switch, the "torpedo-bomb-smoke tank" switch and the bomb-torpedo R.P. switch.

(*c*) MARK 8 GUNSIGHT.—The Mark 8 illuminated gunsight provided in this airplane is used for glide bombing. It is located in a recess in the cowling forward of the pilot's instrument panel and aft of the windshield on the centerline of the fuselage. The control panel is mounted below the distribution panel.

(*d*) BOMB RELEASE BUTTON.—The pilot's Bomb Release Button is located on the aft top of the control stick and is marked with the raised letter "B". This button when pressed, will release the smoke tank, the torpedo and any of the bombs which may be loaded in the bomb bay. The bombs may be released either "select or train", depending on the setting of the bomber's "select-train" switch.

Note

Only the pilot can release the smoke tank and the torpedo.

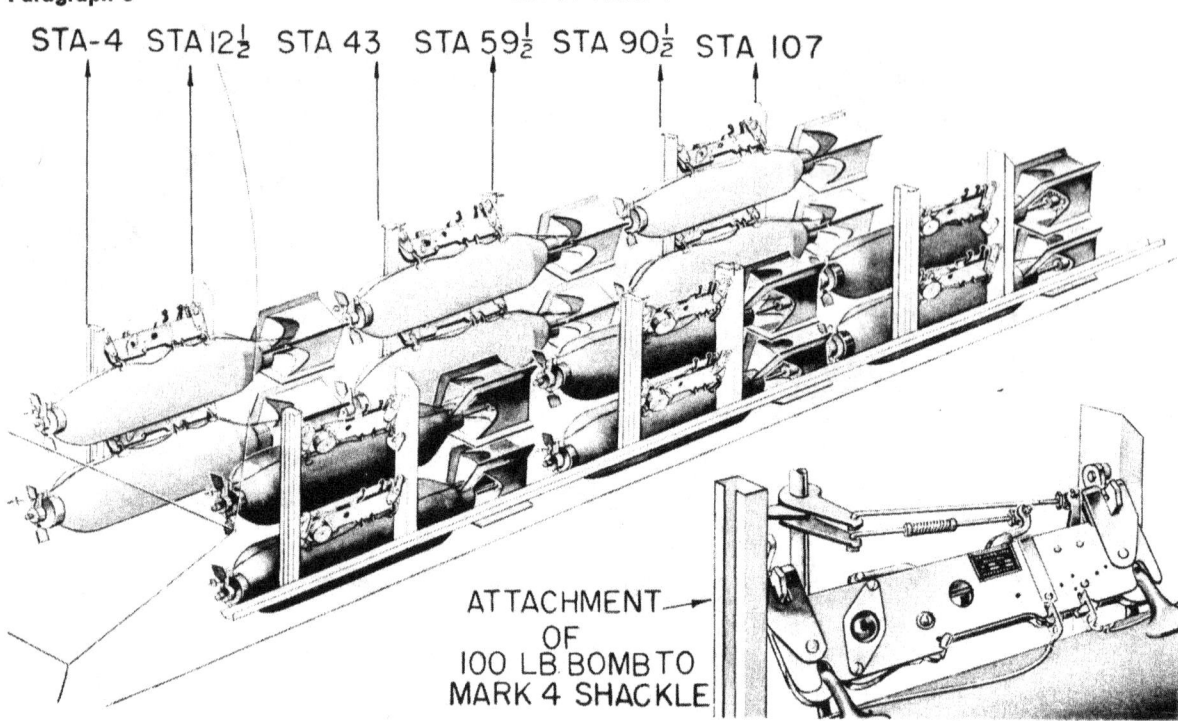

Figure 78 — 100-Lb. Bomb Installation

(e) EMERGENCY BOMB RELEASE HANDLE. On TBM-3 airplanes (Navy Serial 22857 to 23656, 68062 to 69184 inclusive) employing Mark 4 shackles the emergency bomb release handle is located on the pilot's starboard instrument panel. On TBM-3 airplanes (Navy Serial 69185 and subsequent) employing Mark 8 shackles the emergency bomb release handle is located on the pilot's sub-instrument panel. This handle serves the same function in both the Mark 4 and Mark 8 installations and when pulled by the pilot releases the entire bomb load. In case of failure of the electrical bomb release system this control provides the pilot with a positive method of releasing the bomb load.

(2) BOMBARDIER'S CONTROLS.

(a) BOMB BAY DOOR CONTROL HANDLE. This handle is located on the port side of the forward bulkhead of the bombardier's compartment and enables the bombardier to open the bomb bay doors if the necessity arises.

(b) BOMBARDIER'S ELECTRICAL PANEL.—The bombardier's electrical panel is mounted on the port side of the forward section of the compartment. This panel contains the following electrical controls for the bombing equipment; light rheostats, light switches, bombing selector switches, circuit breakers, and jewel warning lights. The panel is energized when the pilot's Armament Master Switch is in the ON position. The Armament Power Indicator will light, thus indicating to the bombardier that this connection exists.

(c) STATION DISTRIBUTOR.—An SD-1 station distributor is located on the port side of the bombardier's compartment. This unit is set to control the sequence in which bombs are released. After the first bomb selected on distributor dial is released, it resets the circuit for releasing the next bomb in line. Always set the station distributor at the lowest station number at which a bomb is carried.

    100 lb. bombs set at No. 1
    500 lb. bombs set at No. 9
    1000 lb. AP bombs set at No. 7
    1000 lb. GP bomb set at No. 8
    1600 lb. AP bomb set at No. 8
    2000 lb. GP bomb set at No. 8
    1000 lb. GP bombs in tandem set at No. 10
    Torpedo set at No. 13

(d) INTERVALOMETER.—The intervalometer is installed on the port side of the bombardier's compartment. This instrument can be actuated by the pilot's bomb release button or bombardier's firing key. The function of the intervalometer is to space the dropping of bombs in train.

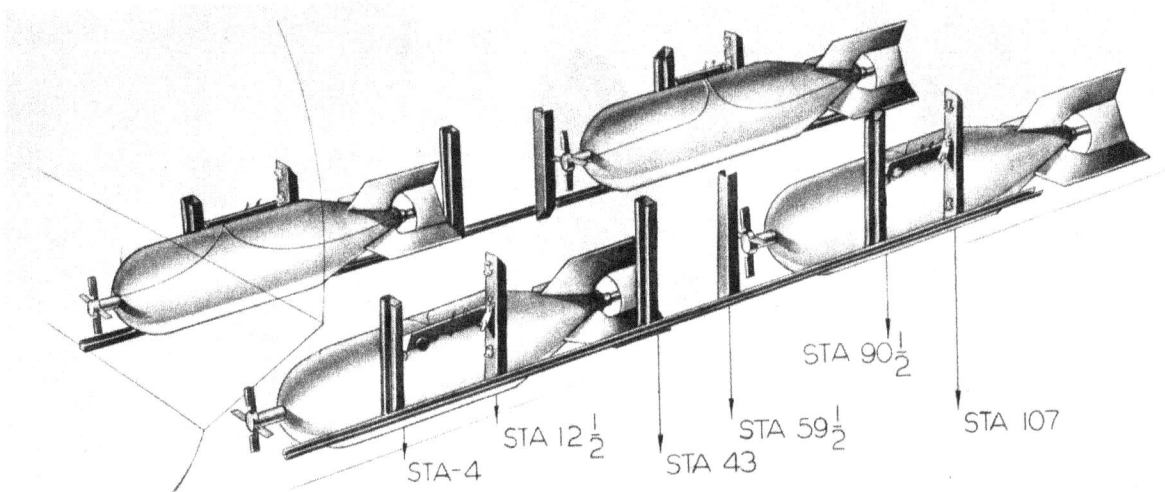

Figure 79 — 500-Lb. Bomb Installation

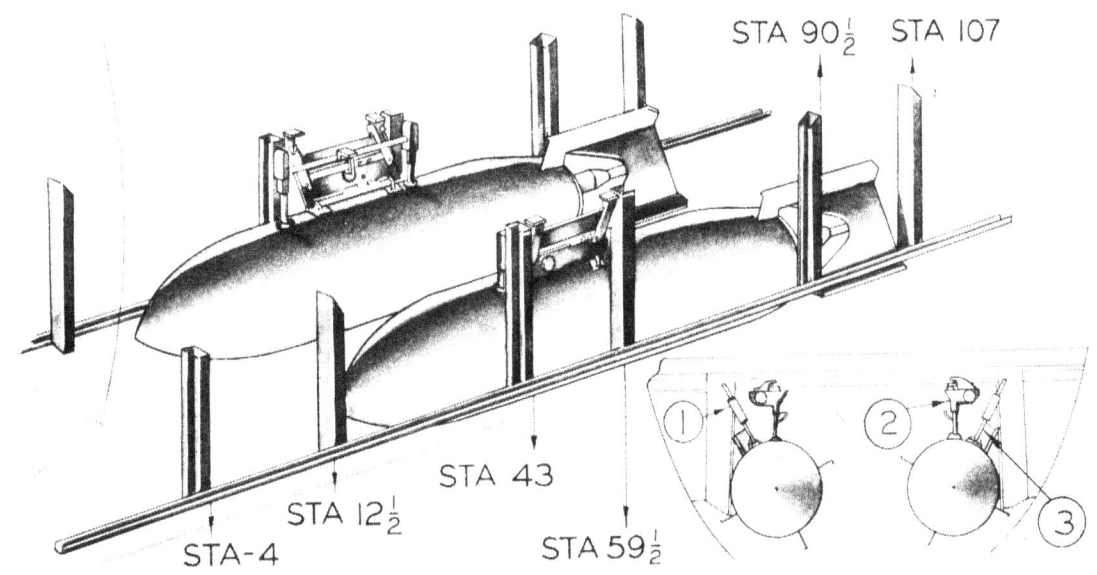

1. Bomb Shackle Extension
2. Hoist and Brace
3. Bomb Shackle

Figure 80 — 1000-Lb. Bomb Installation

(f) ARM-SAFE LEVER.—This lever is used only on those TBM airplanes designed for Mark 4 shackles. The lever is located on the starboard side of the bombardier's compartment and must be in the ARM position before the bomb shackles will release electrically.

(g) FIRING KEY.—The bombardier's firing key has a lead wire of sufficient length to permit the bombardier to hold it in his hand during bombing operations. There is a clip above the electrical panel where it may be stowed when not in use.

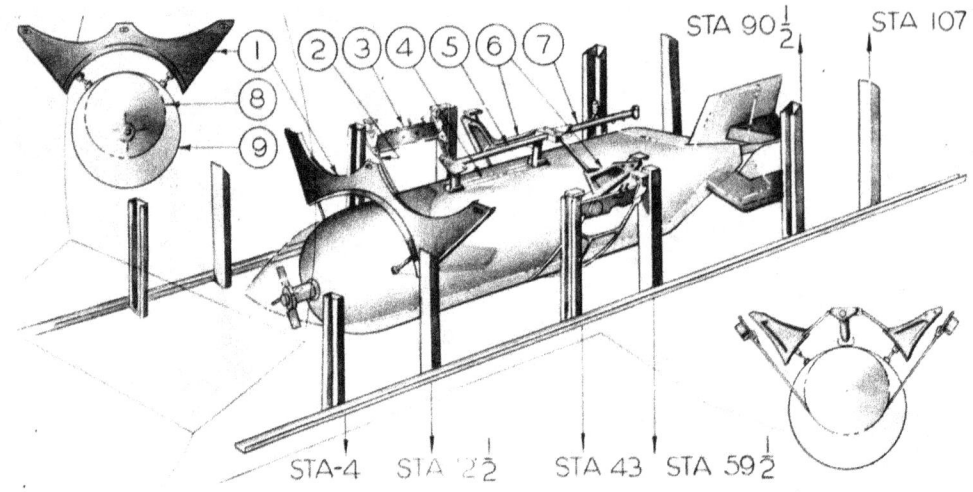

1 Front Sway Brace
2 Sling
3 Shackle
4 Fitting
5 Rack Installation
6 Rear Sway Brace
7 Drag Brace Assembly
8 1600 lb. Bomb
9 1000 lb. Bomb

Figure 81 — 1000- and 1600-Lb. Bomb Installation

c. OPERATION.

(1) BOMB BAY DOORS.

(*a*) The pilot opens the bomb bay doors by pushing the bomb door control handle to the DOWN position. Pulling the handle UP closes the doors.

(*b*) The bombardier opens the bomb bay doors by pulling the bomb door control handle "AFT". Pushing the handle FORWARD closes the doors.

Note

Neither electrical nor manual bomb and torpedo controls will function unless the bomb bay doors are fully open.

(2) PILOT'S CONTROLS.

(*a*) TORPEDO.—The torpedo is released electrically or manually by the pilot. The manual release is accomplished by pulling the emergency bomb release handle. The electrical release requires the following steps after the bomb bay doors have been opened.

1. Set the Bomb-Torpedo Switch in the Torpedo position.

2. Set the Bomb-Torpedo-R.P. switch in Bomb-Torpedo position.

3. On those TBM airplanes employing Mark 4 shackles, direct the bombardier to unlock the bomb shackles by setting the Arm-Safe Lever in Arm Tail or Arm Nose and Tail position. On TBM airplanes employing Mark 8 shackles this step is eliminated.

4. Close the pilot's Armament Master Switch.

5. Press and release the Bomb Release Button on the control stick, to release the torpedo.

6. Close the bomb bay doors.

(*b*) BOMBS.—The bombs may be released either electrically or manually by the pilot. The electrical release requires the following steps after the bomb bay doors have been opened.

1. Set the Bomb-Torpedo switch in Bomb position.

2. Set the Bomb-Torpedo-R.P. switch in Bomb-Torpedo position.

3. Direct the bombardier to set the Select-Train switch of the Intervalometer to Select for one bomb or to Train for bombs in train and the Station Distributor for bomb stations used.

4. On those TBM airplanes employing Mark 4 shackles direct the bombardier to unlock the bomb shackles by setting the Arm Safe lever to Armed Tail or Armed Nose and Tail position as required. On TBM airplanes employing Mark 8 shackles direct the bombardier to set the Bomb Arming Switches on the bombardier's electrical panel to Armed Tail or Armed Nose and Tail position as required.

5. Close the pilot's Armament Master Switch.

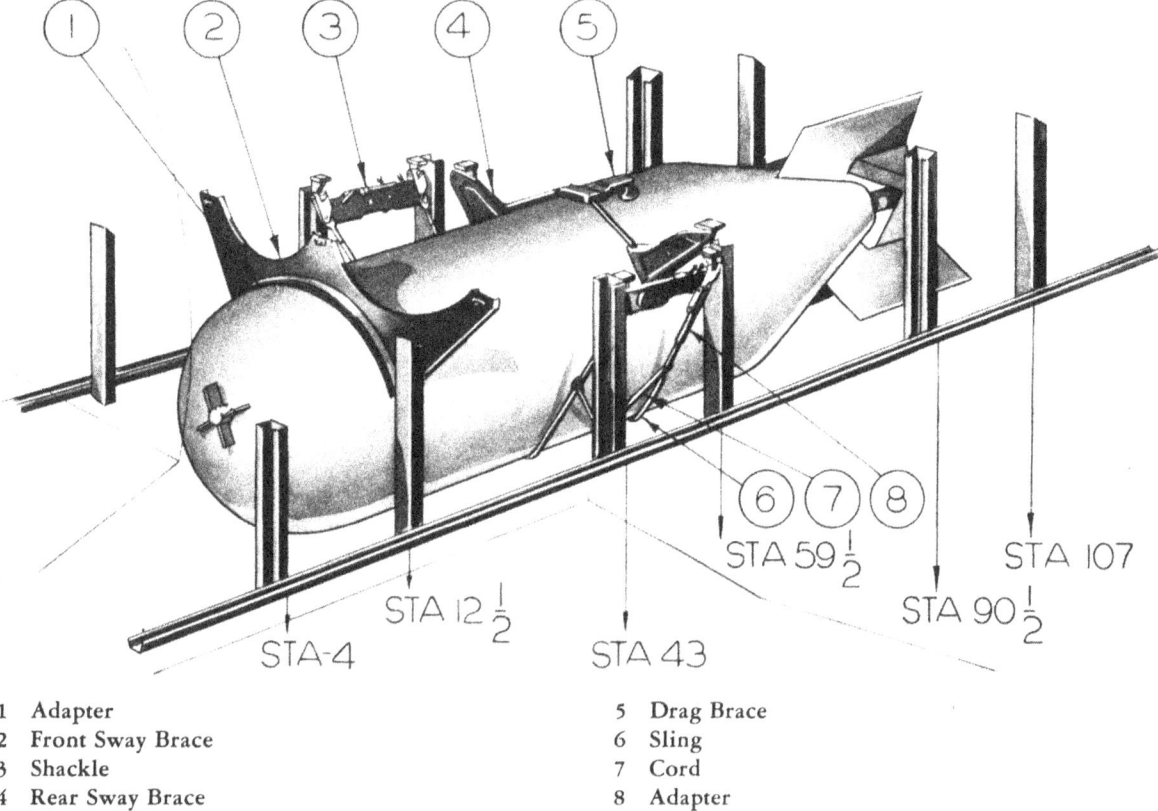

1 Adapter
2 Front Sway Brace
3 Shackle
4 Rear Sway Brace
5 Drag Brace
6 Sling
7 Cord
8 Adapter

Figure 82 — 2000-Lb. Bomb Installation

6. Press and release the Bomb Release Button on the control stick to release bombs.

7. Close the bomb bay doors.

WARNING

In the event that entire bomb load is not dropped the Arm-Safe lever should be moved to Safe position immediately after the dropping of partial bomb load. Bombs in the Armed condition constitute a hazard to safe landings. If bombs are being released in train no attempt should be made to close the bomb bay doors until it is definitely certain that all bombs have been released.

(3) BOMBARDIER'S CONTROLS.—The bombardier can release the bombs electrically with his firing key in case of emergency.

(a) ELECTRICAL RELEASE.—The electrical release requires the following steps after the bomb bay doors have been opened and the bombardier's panel has been energized by the pilot, who closes the Armament Master Switch. The bombardier is notified that the bombardier's panel has been energized by the illumination of the Armament Power Indicator.

1. Attach the firing key cable to the receptacle, located under the bombardier's electric panel.

2. Close the Manual-Automatic switch by setting it to the "Manual" position.

3. Set the Select-Train switch of the intervalometer to Select or Train to control the number of bombs to be released and the interval of release.

4. Set the station distributor to the position required for the type of bombs carried.

5. On TBM airplanes employing Mark 4 shackles unlock the bomb shackles by setting the Arm-Safe lever to Armed Tail or Armed Nose and Tail, as required. On TBM airplanes employing Mark 8 shackles set the bomb arming switches on the bombardier's electrical panel to Armed Tail or Armed Nose and Tail position as required.

6. Press and release the bombardier's firing key to release the bombs.

7. Close the bomb bay doors.

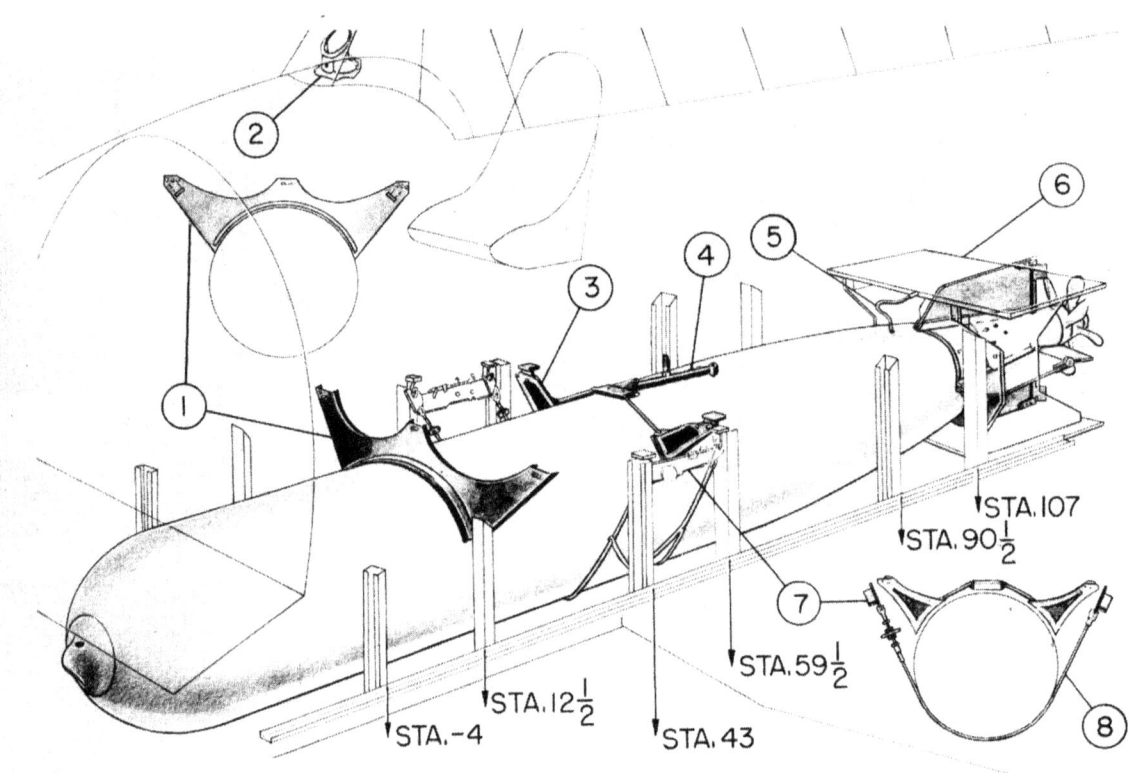

1. Front Sway Brace
2. Mk 8 Gun Sight
3. Rear Sway Brace
4. Brace Assembly
5. Lanyard
6. Torpedo Stabilizer
7. Shackle
8. Sling

Figure 83 — Torpedo Installation

d. GLIDE BOMBING.—The maximum permissible angles for glide bombing operations are given below:

Glide Bombing U.S. Bombs	Maximum Permissible Angle for Glide Bombing
100 lb. class bomb, clearance from airplane structure	30 degrees
100 lb. class bomb, clearance of nose from bomb in shackles ahead. (Provision is made automatically for releasing the lower tier of 100 lb. bombs prior to the upper tier)	35 degrees
500 lb. class bomb, clearance from structure of airplane	20 degrees
1000 lb. class bomb, clearance from structure of airplane	63 degrees
1600 lb. class bomb, clearance from structure of airplane	66 degrees

Note

Condensed Bombing and Armament Operating Instructions are included in the Pilot's Chart Board in later model TBM-3 airplanes.

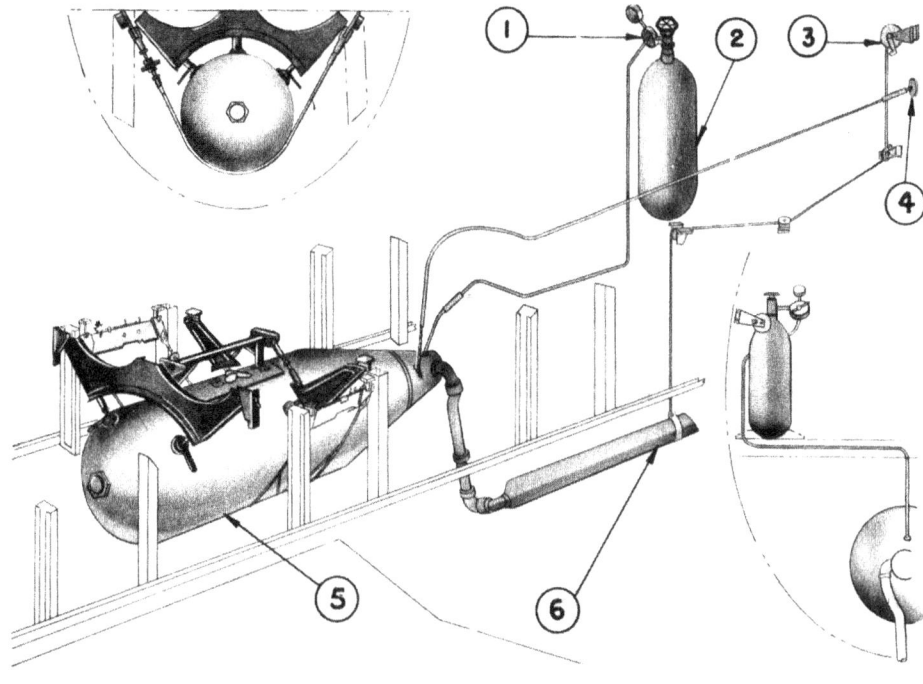

1 Regulator Assembly	4 Control Handle
2 Smoke Tank Bottle	5 Smoke Tank
3 Exhaust Pipe Reel	6 Exhaust Tube

Figure 84 — Smoke Tank Installation

9 HEATING AND VENTILATING.

a. GENERAL.—The first 458 TBM-3 airplanes (Navy Serial No. 22857 to 23313) are equipped with two Janitrol gasoline heaters, mounted one above the other on the starboard side of the fuselage aft of the second cockpit. The upper unit heats the pilot's cockpit while the lower one heats the bombardier's compartment. Air is taken in through a scoop on the lower right wing surface and is directed through ducts into the heaters.

Airplanes (Navy Serial Nos. 23314 to 23656, 68062 to 69538, 85459 to 85780) are equipped with a single upper heater to heat the pilot's cockpit. No provision is made for heaters on Navy Serial No. 85781 and subsequent airplanes.

b. PILOT'S COCKPIT.—The heated air in the pilot's cockpit can be directed to warm the pilot's feet, to heat the cockpit or defrost the windshield.

(1) Set the heater switch, on the distribution panel on the right side of the pilot's cockpit, to the ON position.

(2) Adjust the duct throttle valves, one just below and to the right of the pilot's seat and the other on the floor just below the instrument panel on the right side of the cockpit, to direct air where desired.

c. BOMBARDIER'S COMPARTMENT.

(1) Set the heater switch, on the bombardier's control panel, to the ON position.

(2) Adjust the duct throttle valves to direct air to the turret or bombardier's compartment.

d. VENTILATION.—The system can be used for cold air ventilation with the heater switch OFF.

10. MISCELLANEOUS EQUIPMENT.

a. TOW TARGET.

(1) STREAM TARGET.—With the bomb doors open, pull the "IN TOW" handle, located in the lower left side of the pilot's cockpit, to release the towing cable and the target sleeve from the container. The bomb doors may be closed after sleeve and cable are clear.

(2) DROP TARGET.—Pull the release handle, located on the bombardier's compartment floor. This releases the towing cable and the target sleeve.

b. SMOKE TANK.

(1) GENERAL. — The smoke screen tank is carried in the bomb bay. A handle, which controls the gate valve on the tank outlet, is installed on the bracket adjacent to the reel on the left side of the bombardier's compartment.

(2) TO LAY SMOKE SCREEN.

(a) Unwind the exhaust pipe control reel.

(b) Pull the smoke tank control handle to open the tank gate valve. Rotate the handle to "LOCK".

(c) Regulate the control valve on the CO_2 cylinder for the desired quality of the smoke screen.

(3) RELEASING THE SMOKE TANK ELECTRICALLY.

(a) Shut the CO_2 cylinder control valve.

(b) Open the bomb doors.

(c) Set the bomb-torpedo-smoke tank switch on the pilot's distribution panel to the SMOKE TANK position.

(e) The pilot then throws the Armament Master Switch on the distribution panel to ON.

(f) Press the bomb release switch on the control stick.

(4) MANUAL SMOKE TANK RELEASE.

(a) Open the bomb bay doors.

(b) Pull the emergency Bomb Release handle.

Note

The smoke tank can be released only by the pilot.

c. PYROTECHNICS.

Eight AN Mark 4 float lights are carried in racks in the rear of the bombardier's compartment.

d. CHARTBOARD.

The chartboard is stowed directly below and forward of the main instrument panel. It can be positioned for use by unfastening the catch and sliding the board toward the rear of the cockpit.

e. RELIEF TUBES.

The pilot's relief tube is located below the pilot's seat on the port side. The turret gunner's and bombardier's relief tube is located below the turret on the starboard side of the bombardier's electrical panel.

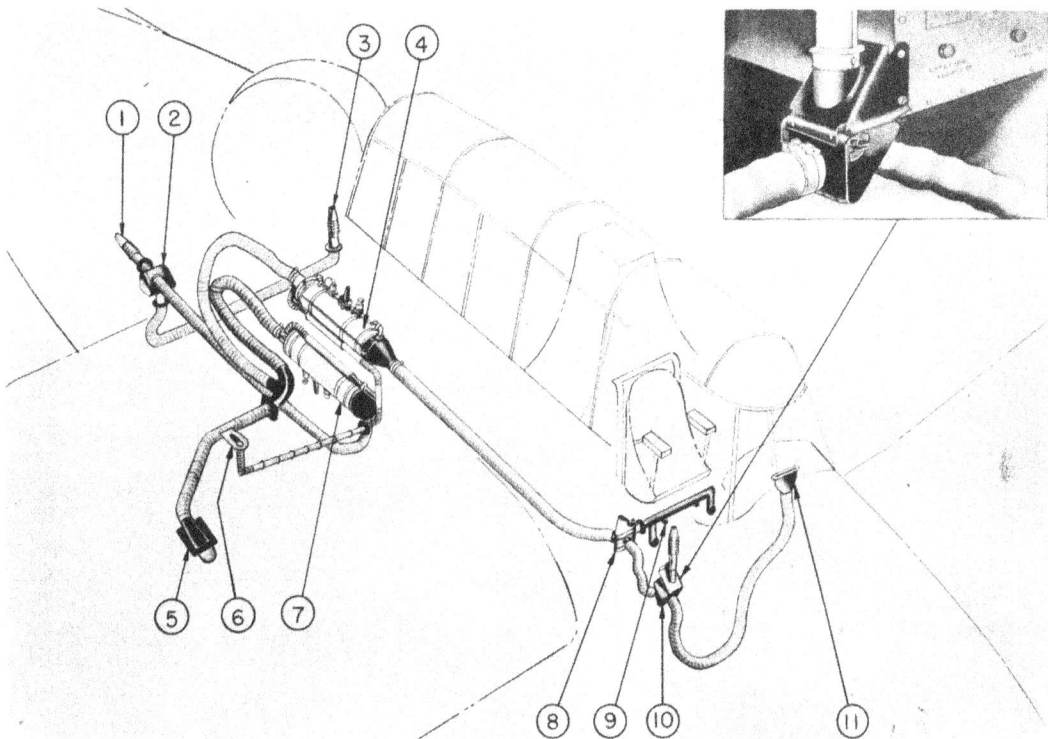

1. Bombardier's Nozzle
2. Air Control Valve
3. Turret Gunner's Nozzle
4. Pilot's Cockpit Heater
5. Air Scoop
6. Exhaust Outlet
7. Bombardier's Heater
8. Pilot's Air Control Valve
9. Foot Warmer
10. Pilot's Control Valve and Nozzle
11. Windshield Defroster

Figure 84A—Heater Installation, Earlier Model Airplanes

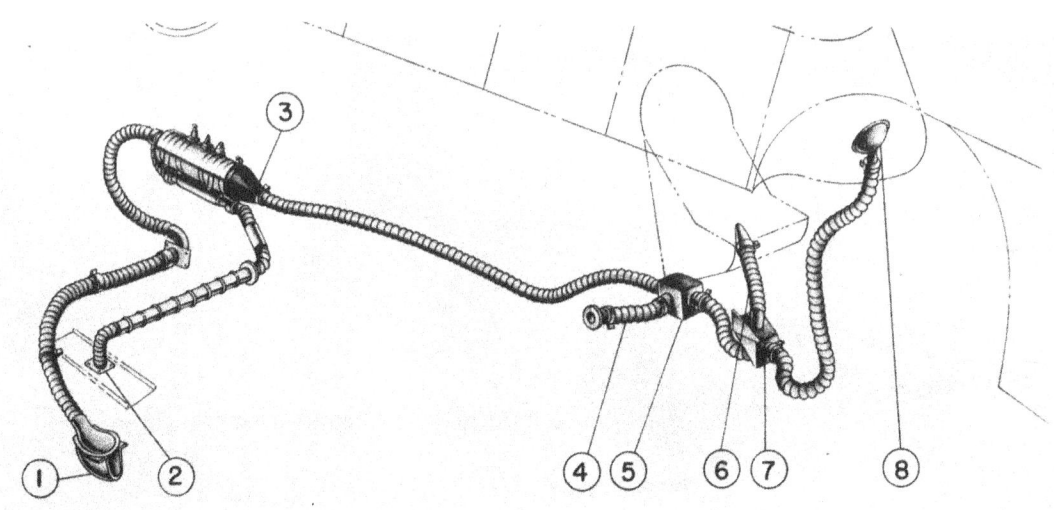

1. Air Scoop
2. Exhaust Outlet
3. Heater
4. By-Pass Outlet
5. By-Pass Control Valve
6. Pilot's Cockpit Nozzle
7. Pilot's Control Valve
8. Windshield Defroster

Figure 84B—Heater Installation, Later Model Airplanes

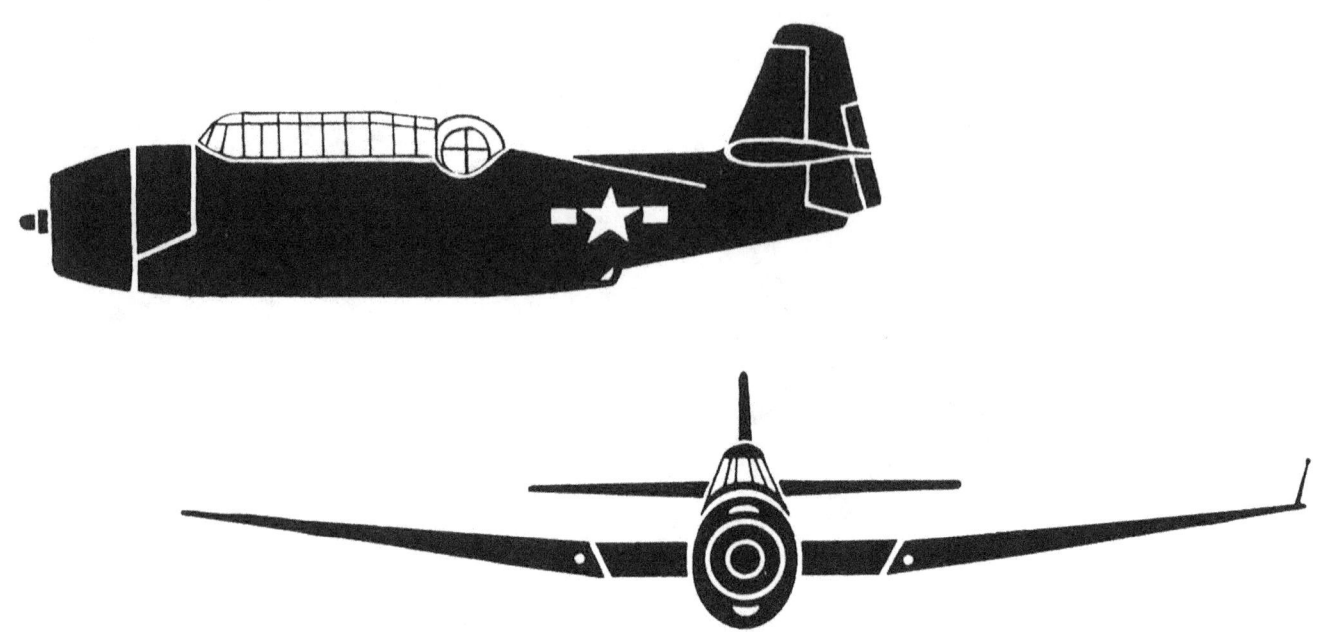

THIS PAGE INTENTIONALLY LEFT BLANK.

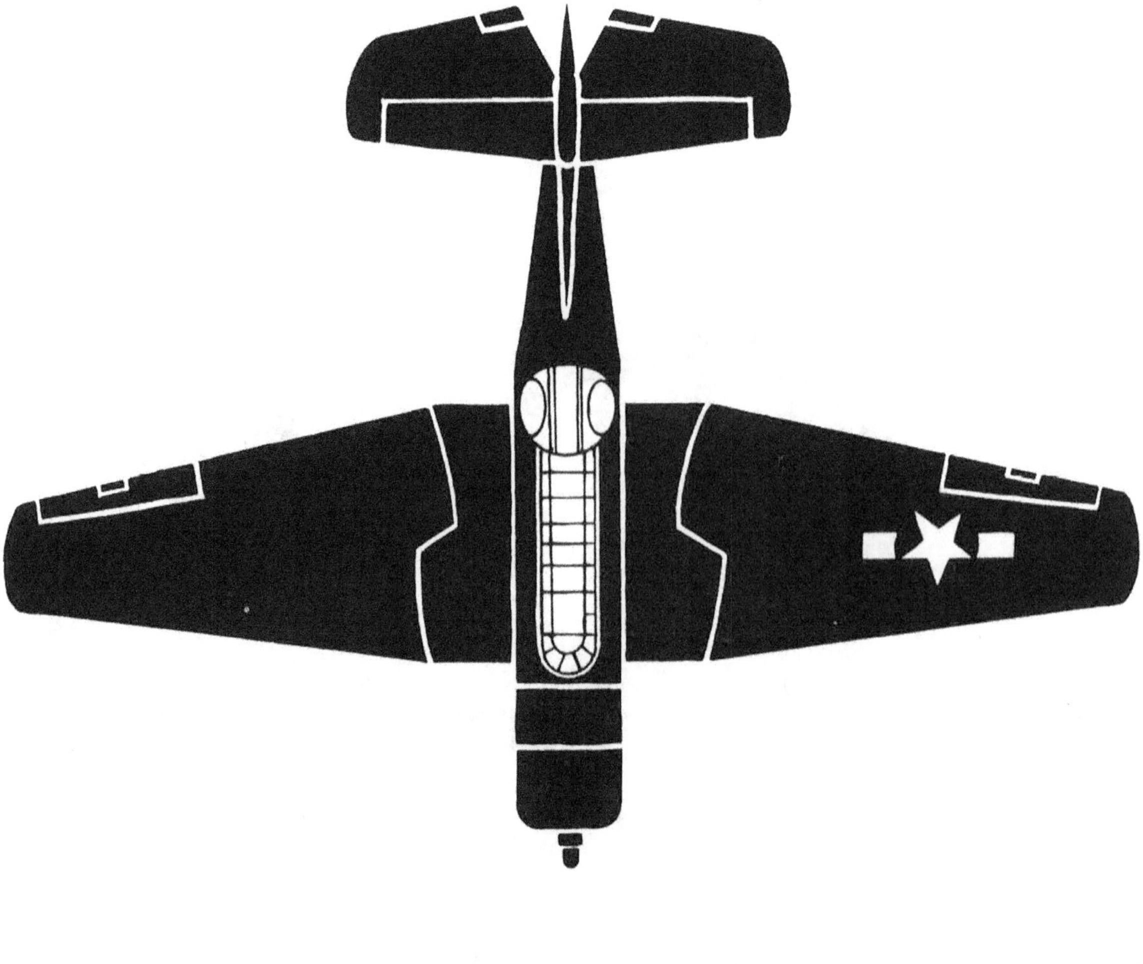

Appendix I

AN 01-190EB-1

"Appendix I of this publication shall not be carried in aircraft on combat missions or when there is a reasonable chance of its falling into the hands of the enemy."

TAKE-OFF, CLIMB & LANDING CHART

AIRCRAFT MODEL(S):   ENGINE MODEL(S):

TAKE-OFF DISTANCE — FEET

GROSS WEIGHT LB.	HEAD WIND		HARD SURFACE RUNWAY						SOD-TURF RUNWAY						SOFT SURFACE RUNWAY					
			AT SEA LEVEL		AT 3000 FEET		AT 6000 FEET		AT SEA LEVEL		AT 3000 FEET		AT 6000 FEET		AT SEA LEVEL		AT 3000 FEET		AT 6000 FEET	
	M.P.H.	KTS.	GROUND RUN	TO CLEAR 50' OBJ.	GROUND RUN	TO CLEAR 50' OBJ.	GROUND RUN	TO CLEAR 50' OBJ.	GROUND RUN	TO CLEAR 50' OBJ.	GROUND RUN	TO CLEAR 50' OBJ.	GROUND RUN	TO CLEAR 50' OBJ.	GROUND RUN	TO CLEAR 50' OBJ.	GROUND RUN	TO CLEAR 50' OBJ.	GROUND RUN	TO CLEAR 50' OBJ.
14,500	0	0	790		865		930		795		875		955		830		920		995	
	17	15	440		525		590		475		545		605		495		565		625	
	29	25	320		360		420		330		375		430		340		390		495	
15,500	0	0	910		995		1080		925		1020		1115		965		1070		1160	
	17	15	525		620		690		565		640		715		590		665		740	
	29	25	380		430		500		395		445		515		405		465		530	
16,500	0	0	1030		1145		1240		1070		1175		1275		1115		1225		1340	
	17	15	620		720		800		655		745		830		690		775		865	
	29	25	445		505		580		460		525		600		480		550		630	
18,000	0	0	1245		1365		1500		1295		1430		1550		1360		1495		1635	
	17	15	770		895		995		815		925		1030		855		970		1090	
	29	25	565		635		725		585		660		750		615		695		795	

NOTE: INCREASE CHART DISTANCES AS FOLLOWS: 75°F + 10%; 100°F + 20%; 125°F + 30%; 190°F + 40%
DATA AS OF 12/11/44   BASED ON: FLIGHT TEST AT 14,800# AND 16,900#   OPTIMUM TAKE-OFF WITH 2800 RPM, 49 IN.HG. 8 3/4   FLAP IS 80% OF CHART VALUES

CLIMB DATA

GROSS WEIGHT LB.	AT SEA LEVEL				AT 6000 FEET				AT 12,000 FEET				AT 16,000 FEET				AT 20000 FEET				AT 25000 FEET			
	BEST I.A.S.		RATE OF CLIMB F.P.M.	GAL. OF FUEL USED	BEST I.A.S.		RATE OF CLIMB F.P.M.	FROM SEA LEVEL	BEST I.A.S.		RATE OF CLIMB F.P.M.	FROM SEA LEVEL	BEST I.A.S.		RATE OF CLIMB F.P.M.	FROM SEA LEVEL	BEST I.A.S.		RATE OF CLIMB F.P.M.	FROM SEA LEVEL	BEST I.A.S.		RATE OF CLIMB F.P.M.	FROM SEA LEVEL
	MPH	KTS			MPH	KTS		TIME MIN. / FUEL USED	MPH	KTS		TIME MIN. / FUEL USED	MPH	KTS		TIME MIN. / FUEL USED	MPH	KTS		TIME MIN. / FUEL USED	MPH	KTS		TIME MIN. / FUEL USED
14,500	140	122	800	30	135	118	1650	3.5 / 41	130	113	1250	7.5 / 52	127	110	1150	11.0 / 62	124	108	850	15.0 / 73	120	105	500	21.5 / 87
15,500	140	122	650	30	135	118	1500	4.0 / 42	130	113	1100	8.5 / 55	127	110	950	12.5 / 66	124	108	700	17.5 / 80	120	105	350	26.5 / 100
16,500	140	122	1450	30	135	118	1350	4.5 / 44	130	113	900	9.5 / 58	127	110	800	14.5 / 72	124	108	550	20.5 / 88	120	105	150	35.0 / 118
18,000	140	122	1250	30	135	118	1100	5.5 / 47	130	113	700	12.0 / 65	127	110	550	18.0 / 82	124	108	300	27.0 / 106			—	—

POWER PLANT SETTINGS: DETAILS ON FIG.   SECTION III):
DATA AS OF 12/11/44   BASED ON: FUEL USED (U.S. GAL.) (INCLUDES WARM-UP & TAKE-OFF ALLOWANCE)

LANDING DISTANCE — FEET

GROSS WEIGHT LB.	BEST IAS APPROACH				HARD DRY SURFACE						FIRM DRY SOD						WET OR SLIPPERY					
	POWER OFF		POWER ON		AT SEA LEVEL		AT 3000 FEET		AT 6000 FEET		AT SEA LEVEL		AT 3000 FEET		AT 6000 FEET		AT SEA LEVEL		AT 3000 FEET		AT 6000 FEET	
	MPH	KTS	MPH	KTS	GROUND ROLL	TO CLEAR 50' OBJ.	GROUND ROLL	TO CLEAR 50' OBJ.	GROUND ROLL	TO CLEAR 50' OBJ.	GROUND ROLL	TO CLEAR 50' OBJ.	GROUND ROLL	TO CLEAR 50' OBJ.	GROUND ROLL	TO CLEAR 50' OBJ.	GROUND ROLL	TO CLEAR 50' OBJ.	GROUND ROLL	TO CLEAR 50' OBJ.	GROUND ROLL	TO CLEAR 50' OBJ.
15,750	98	85	85	74	1100		1190		1300		1200		1320		1435		2620		2880		3130	
12,500	87	76	75	65	855		925		1030		945		1020		1140		2080		2240		2480	

DATA AS OF 12/11/44   BASED ON: CALCULATIONS WITH POWER OFF LANDING

REMARKS:
NOTE: TO DETERMINE FUEL CONSUMPTION IN BRITISH IMPERIAL GALLONS, MULTIPLY BY 10, THEN DIVIDE BY 12

LEGEND:
I.A.S.: INDICATED AIRSPEED
M.P.H.: MILES PER HOUR
KTS.: KNOTS
F.P.M.: FEET PER MINUTE

Figure 85 — Take-off, Climb, and Landing Chart

Appendix I

AN 01-190EB-1

FLIGHT OPERATION INSTRUCTION CHART.—This chart includes information concerning range attainable and recommended power plant control settings for various combinations of gross weight, fuel load, altitude and air speed. To avoid misuse or misrepresentation of the charts, cognizance should be taken of the following:

1. The charted ranges make no allowance for warm-up, take-off and climb. Fuel consumed during these operations should be obtained from take-off, climb and landing chart. Similarly no account is taken of the improved miles per gallon realizable during descent. Neglect of this latter factor is recommended to balance the fuel required for the landing operation.

2. The operating data included on any one chart should be used only when the gross weight is within the limits specified in the title block. When diminished fuel load causes the gross weight to decrease to a value included in the weight limits of the preceding chart, the operating data included in the corresponding column of that chart should be used. THIS IS ESSENTIAL, AS RANGES HAVE BEEN COMPUTED ON THIS BASIS.

3. When gross weight is within the chart weight limits and less than the maximum (due to lighter initial weight or diminished fuel load) the air speed should be slightly greater than that listed on the chart. To be conservative, no account has been taken of this factor.

4. Experience has indicated that it is necessary to reduce flight test range data by 5 percent to take account of variations in service airplanes and operating techniques. These allowances have been made on the Flight Operation Chart by a corresponding increase in fuel consumption. No ALLOWANCE HAS BEEN MADE FOR WIND, NAVIGATIONAL ERROR OR OTHER CONTINGENCIES. NO ALLOWANCE HAS BEEN MADE FOR COMBAT NOR FORMATION FLIGHT. APPROPRIATE ALLOWANCES FOR THESE ITEMS SHOULD BE DICTATED BY LOCAL DOCTRINE. The fuel quantity used in entering the chart, therefore, should be the fuel available after reaching flight altitude less allowances appropriate for the mission.

Appendix I

AN 01-190EB-1

Figure 86 — Flight Operating Instruction Chart (Sheet 1 of 4 Sheets)

Appendix I

AN 01-190EB-1

FLIGHT OPERATION INSTRUCTION CHART

Figure 86 — Flight Operating Instruction Chart (Sheet 2 of 4 Sheets)

Appendix I

AN 01-190EB-1

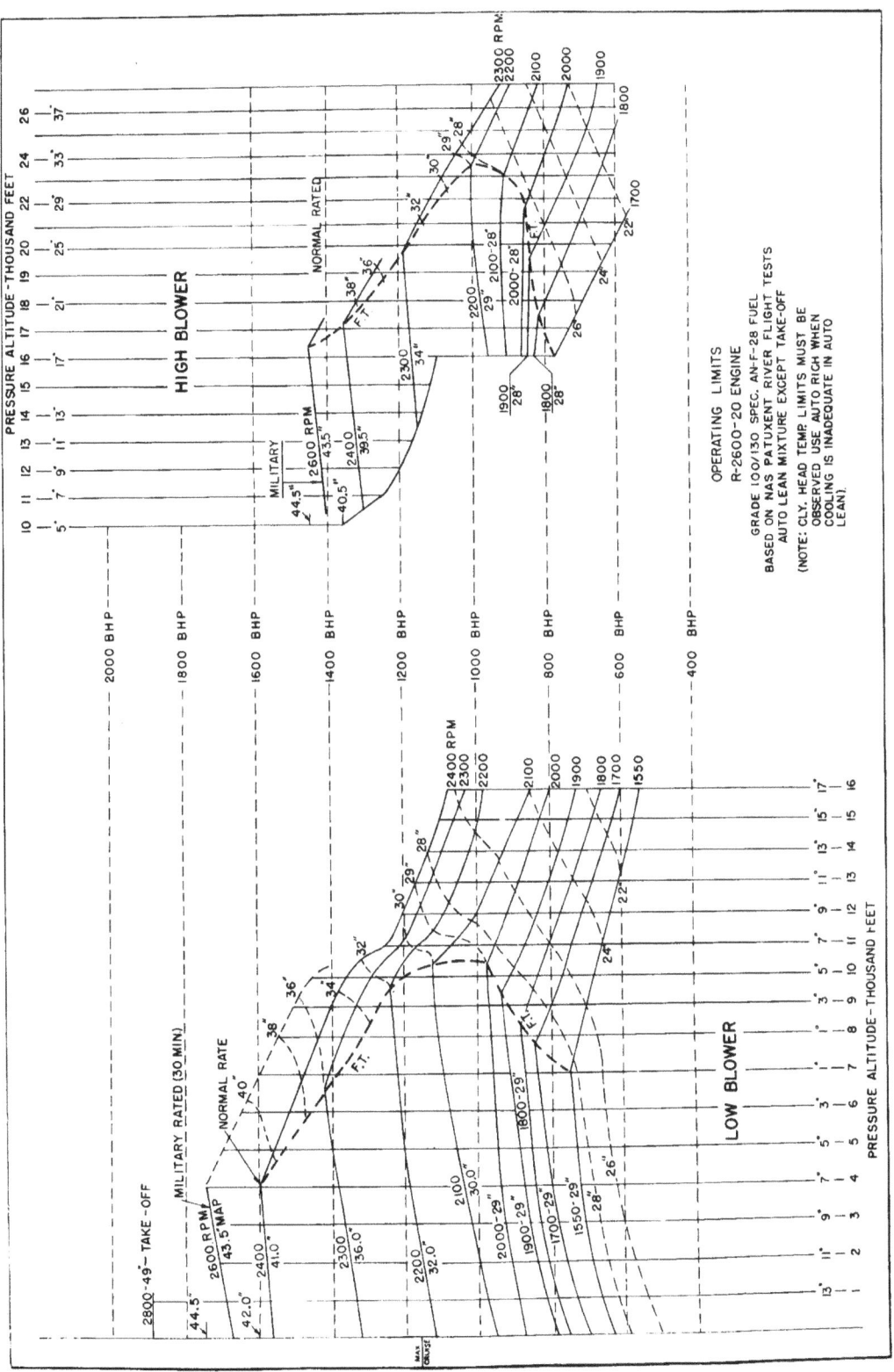

Figure 87—Engine Calibration Curve

ENGINE CALIBRATION CHART

EXAMPLES OF USE

These curves can be used to set operating conditions or to determine engine power at any operating condition within the recommended operating limits of the engine. The curves to the left are for LOW blower operation; the curves to the right are for HIGH blower operation. The horizontal dot-dash line indicates the limit for LEAN mixture operation. Use RICH mixture above this line. Part throttle conditions are those to the left of the oblique heavy dashed line in both the LOW and HIGH blower sections; full throttle conditions are those to the right of these lines.

HIGH POWER—(Part Throttle)

1. When high power climb is desired, operate along one of the constant manifold pressure-RPM lines (sloping lines labeled with manifold pressure and RPM). For constant rated power climb use 41″ Hg. at S.L. decreasing to 40″ Hg. at 4500 feet.

2. Select level flight condition from a point on one of the designated lines, or, if an intermediate condition is desired, any manifold pressure-RPM combination represented in the full throttle portions of the chart can be used for part throttle operation.

CRUISING POWER—(Part Throttle)

1. For power conditions below the dot-dash line, the maximum recommended manifold pressures are independent of RPM.

TO DETERMINE HORSEPOWER—Any Power Condition.

1. Knowing RPM and manifold pressure, spot the condition in the full throttle portion of the section of the chart for the blower ratio in which the engine is operating.

2. Draw a line through the point determined parallel to the constant manifold pressure-RPM lines shown. Read HP at the intersection of this line with the observed pressure altitude.

PRESSURE ALTITUDE.

1. Determine the amount the barometric pressure (altimeter window reading) is above or below 29.92″ Hg.

2. Add 100 feet for each 0.1″ Hg. below 29.92. Subtract 100 feet for each 0.1″ Hg. above 29.92.

Appendix I

AN 01-190EB-1

NO EXTERNAL LOAD ITEMS
AUTO LEAN MIXTURE

TBM-3 LONG RANGE CHART

LOW BLOWER
COWL FLAPS CLOSED

GW 18000 LBS 135 KTS			GW 16000 LBS 125 KTS			DENSITY ALTITUDE	STD. TEMP. °C	GW 14000 LBS 125 KTS			GW 12000 LBS 125 KTS		
CAS RPM	MP	GPH	CAS RPM	MP	GPH			CAS RPM	MP	GPH	CAS RPM	MP	GPH
2080	FT	76	1820	FT	60	16000	-17	1700	FT	53	1600	FT	49
1960	FT	70	1710	FT	56	14000	-13	1600	FT	50	1600	22	47
1830	FT	65	1610	FT	53	12000	-9	1600	23	48	1600	22	45
1730	FT	62	1600	25	51	10000	-5	1600	23	46	1600	22.5	44
1630	FT	59	1600	25	48	8000	-1	1600	23.5	45	1600	22.5	43
1600	29	57	1600	25	47	6000	3	1600	24	44	1600	23	42
1610	29	56	1600	26	47	4000	7	1600	24.5	43	1600	23.5	41
1700	29	55	1600	26.5	46	2000	11	1600	25	43	1600	24	40
1820	29	54	1600	27	46	SEA LEVEL	15	1600	25.5	42	1600	24.5	40

ABBREVIATIONS:

GW - Gross Weight, pounds.
CAS - Calibrated Air Speed, Knots
GPH - Gallons Per Hour.

FT - Full Throttle
STD TEMP - Standard Temperature.

TO USE CHART:

1. For best correlation of charted fuel flow values with actual fuel consumption fly at the recommended CAS for long range at the airplane's gross weight. Enter the chart with the DENSITY ALTITUDE being flown (determined with the Mark 8A computer) and read off RPM, MP and GPH. If the desired airspeed is not attained, change the power settings charted in accordance with the rule outlined below.

2. Rule for TBM-3 Long Range Flight - Fly the CAS recommended for the gross weight. Use 1600 RPM and whatever MP is needed to obtain the CAS, up to 29 inches; if the desired airspeed is then not attained use 29 inches (or Full Throttle if 29 inches cannot be obtained) and whatever RPM is necessary, up to 2080 RPM.

3. The above chart is based on TBM-3 flight tests with carburetor PR48A1, setting number 395109. Fuel consumption figures have not been rendered conservative, and are direct results of the tests. Low cylinder head temperatures that may result from operating at recommended long-range settings are not considered harmful.

Figure 82.—TBM-3 Long-Range Chart

85

Epic Battles of WWII

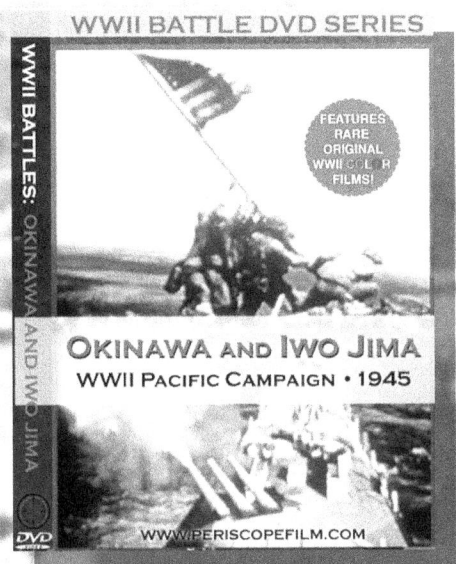

Now Available on DVD!

Aircraft At War DVD Series

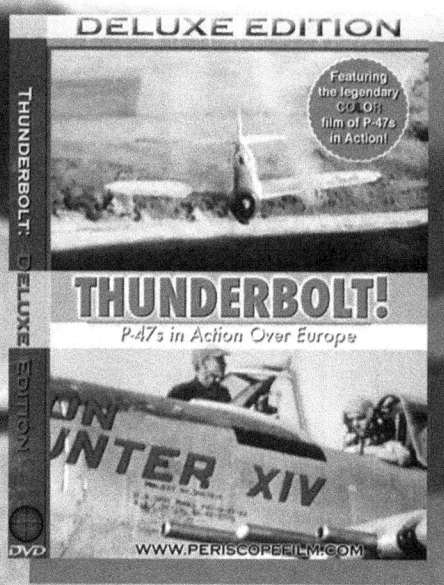
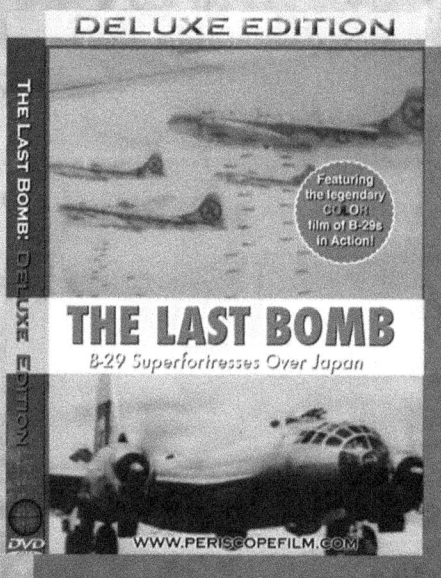
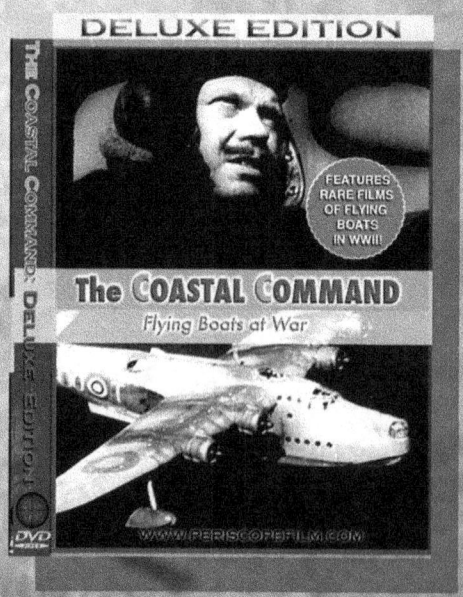

Now Available!

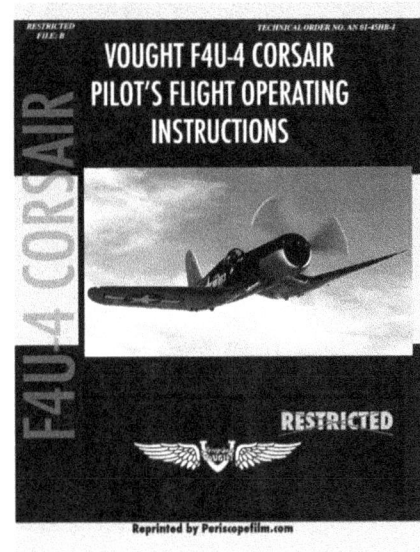
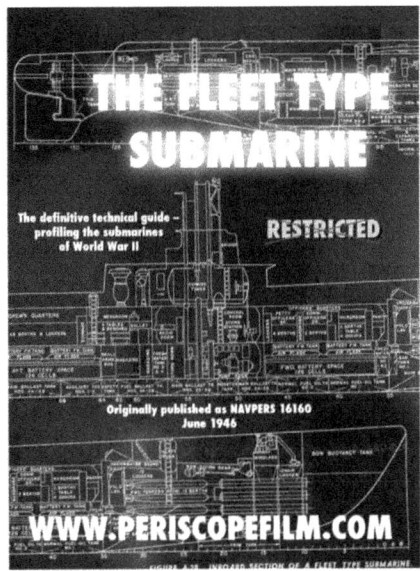
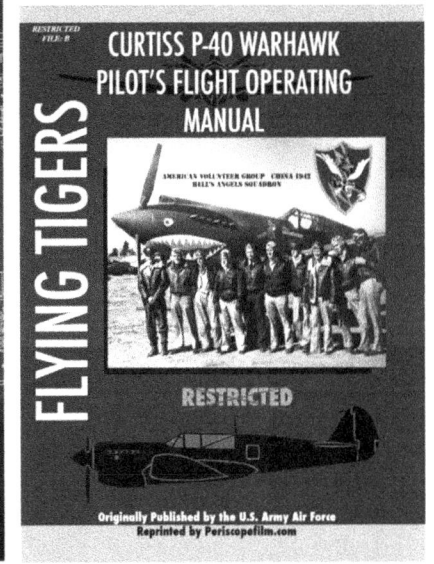

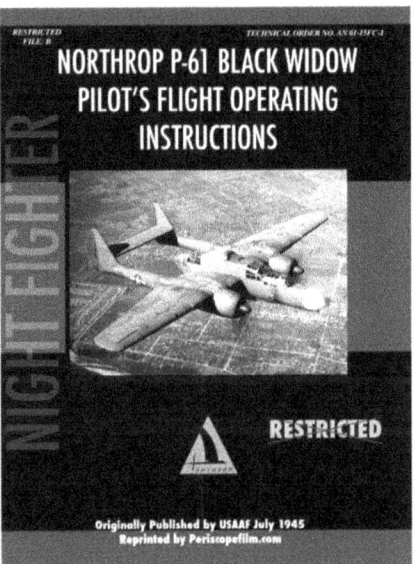

ALSO NOW AVAILABLE FROM PERISCOPEFILM.COM

©2006-2010 PERISCOPE FILM LLC
ALL RIGHTS RESERVED
ISBN #978-1-935700-37-1

WWW.PERISCOPEFILM.COM

www.ingramcontent.com/pod-product-compliance
Lightning Source LLC
LaVergne TN
LVHW061345060426
835512LV00012B/2577